HANDWRITING 6

for Christian Schools® SECOND EDITION

Charlene Killian

Karen L. Wolff

Joyce Garland

Teacher's Edition

Bob Jones University Press • Greenville, South Carolina 29614

Development Consultants
Walter G. Fremont, Ed.D.
Philip D. Smith, Ed.D.
Melva M. Heintz, M.A.
Janice A. Joss, M.A.
Hazel M. Truman, M.A.

NOTE: The fact that materials produced by other publishers may be referred to in this volume does not constitute an endorsement of the content or theological position of materials produced by such publishers. Any references and ancillary materials are listed as an aid to the student or the teacher and in an attempt to maintain the accepted academic standards of the publishing industry.

HANDWRITING 6 Teacher's Edition
Second Edition

Produced in cooperation with the Bob Jones University School of Education and Bob Jones Elementary School.

Developed by
Charlene Killian
Karen L. Wolff

Revision Coordinator
Joyce Garland

Editor
Carolyn Cooper

Revision Graphics
Ellyson Kalagayan
John Bjerk

Illustrator
Ellyson Kalagayan

Graphics
John Bjerk

Computer Formatting
Peggy Hargis

Typesetting
Carla Vogt

Photograph Credits

Cover: George Collins: Lighthouse; Corel Corporation: Space stars, Woman pilot; PhotoDisc, Inc.: Astronomer, Gears, Helicopter, Nurse, Satellite dish; Unusual Films: Xylographer

Pages 4, 14, 23, 31, 39, 48, 57, 65, 73, 81, 89, 97, 105, 112:
Digital Stock: Umpire; PhotoDisc, Inc.: Geologist, Woman pilot; Unusual Films: Xylographer

Photo credits for reduced student pages can be found on page 134.

© 2000 BJU Press
Greenville, South Carolina 29614
First Edition © 1985 BJU Press

Printed in the United States of America

ISBN 978-1-57924-390-6

15 14 13 12 11 10 9 8 7 6 5

Contents

Introduction

Good handwriting is an essential skill—a form of expression and communication. Because handwriting is a complex process that requires a coordinated effort of nearly five hundred muscles, instruction should begin in kindergarten and continue throughout the elementary grades. Accordingly, *HANDWRITING 6 for Christian Schools* seeks to lay a foundation of writing skills on which early learning is broadened and reinforced, not replaced, and to provide proper motivation throughout the elementary grades.

Major Goals

To instill in each student the desire to develop legible, attractive written communication that will glorify the Lord.

To provide good cursive models that show correct letter formation, alignment, neatness, slant, and spacing.

To provide edifying handwriting experiences that reinforce skills in other disciplines.

To establish a foundation of good handwriting that will last a lifetime.

Historical Background

Handwriting instruction reflects the vacillating pendulum of educational philosophy. Teachers in the past spent much time instructing their students in the "whole-arm" technique, popular in the latter part of the nineteenth century. Using this technique, the writer's whole arm moved from the shoulder as he wrote. This movement proved extremely difficult for beginning elementary children whose coordination was not sufficiently developed for this technique. Thus, when teachers began lessons in cursive ("running" or "connected" writing), they also began endless handwriting drills.

And since this technique assumed teaching cursive in the first grade, children had to learn two alphabets—a cursive alphabet for writing and a typeface alphabet for reading.

The twentieth-century response to this technique was twofold. Some teachers eagerly embraced a partial solution—the manuscript alphabet, introduced in 1921. This alphabet, because it looked more like the typeface the students were expected to read, eliminated the necessity of having the students learn two alphabets in first grade. Moreover, since this alphabet took less time to teach and required fewer drills, it rapidly became accepted as the best method for teaching children to write. Other teachers, weary of handwriting drills, stopped teaching handwriting altogether. They argued that students could learn handwriting skills through observation.

Although the manuscript alphabet is popularly accepted today by many educators, it is becoming increasingly apparent throughout the educational system that the manuscript style has several fundamental problems. First, because the letters consist of sticks and circles, children have difficulty forming the letters properly. Making straight stick shapes and round circle shapes are unnatural movements for the writing hand. Forming these shapes properly demands careful drawing motions. Second, children have difficulty remembering where to put the stick in relation to the circle. Many manuscript *b*s become *d*s and many *p*s become *q*s when a child cannot remember on which side of the circle the stick belongs. In addition, connecting the circle and the stick properly requires well-developed motor skills and careful drawing motions.

Third, since most of the letters bear little resemblance to the cursive letters taught later, students must learn a completely different system of movements to form cursive letters. In no other subject is such a drastic change common practice. On the contrary, early skills usually provide the foundation for further and more advanced skill development.

Letter Design

In developing *HANDWRITING for Christian Schools,* Bob Jones University Press followed the guidelines of research to bring the instructional philosophy into balance.

Rationale for Development of BJU Press PreCursive Alphabet

This alphabet corrects the problems inherent in the traditional manuscript and cursive alphabets while retaining the advantages.

1. The PreCursive alphabet capitalizes on the natural movements of a young child's writing hand. Oval shapes replace circles, and slanted lines replace the vertical lines. Rather than drawing, a child begins early to develop a rhythm and a flow which will minimize the transition to cursive writing.

2. Twenty-two of the PreCursive lowercase letters and seventeen of the PreCursive uppercase letters require only one stroke. Fewer stops and starts and decisions aid the child in remembering how to write the letters; a byproduct of this is fewer reversals. Again, the transition to cursive writing is aided.

3. The PreCursive letters look very much like the letters children will see in their reading materials.

Rationale for Development of BJU Press Cursive Alphabet

The specific letter styles adapted for the cursive letters in the HANDWRITING for Christian Schools program were chosen according to the following criteria:

1. Legibility was the dominating consideration in the design of the letters. In adult writing, the letter *b* is the most often misread letter.

2. Uppercase and lowercase letters were kept as similar as possible.

3. PreCursive letters and cursive letters were kept as similar as possible.

4. PreCursive letters were designed so that, with the addition of a cursive joining stroke, the PreCursive becomes the cursive model.

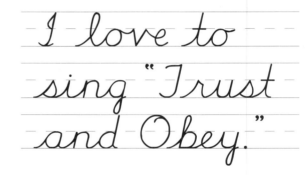

5. Consideration was given to aesthetic design and balance of each letter and to its pleasing appearance in a complete passage of text.

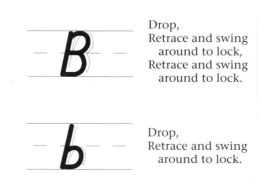

In the fifth and sixth grades, this series also offers several variations of selected uppercase cursive letters. These alternate letters are presented in an effort to renew each student's interest in handwriting and to guide students as they develop individualized handwriting that is both attractive and legible.

PreCursive Stroke Descriptions

Stroke formations

A

(1) Drop left.
(2) Drop right.
(3) Cross.

a

Begin at one,
Swing around to lock,
Retrace and curve.

B

Drop,
Retrace and swing
 around to lock,
Retrace and swing
 around to lock.

b

Drop,
Retrace and swing
 around to lock.

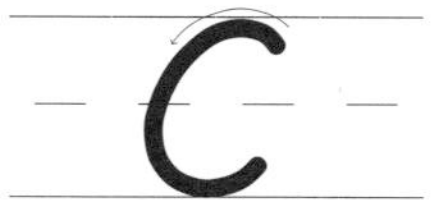

C

Begin at one,
Swing around to five.

c

Begin at one,
Swing around to five.

D

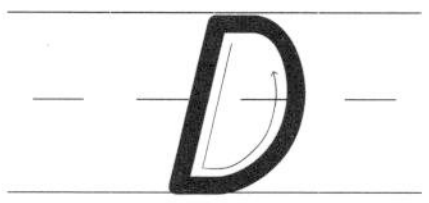

Drop,
Swing around and up
to lock.

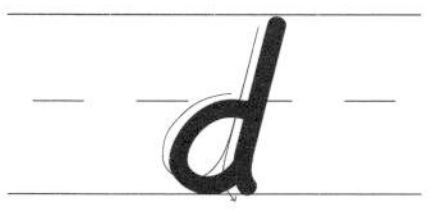

d

Begin at one,
Swing around and up,
Climb high,
Retrace and curve.

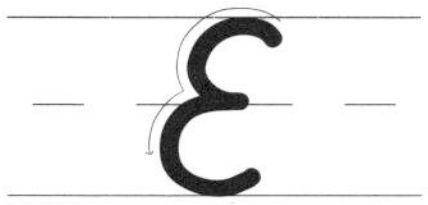

E

Begin at one,
Swerve around toward
three,
Swing around to five.

e

Swing up toward one
and around to five.

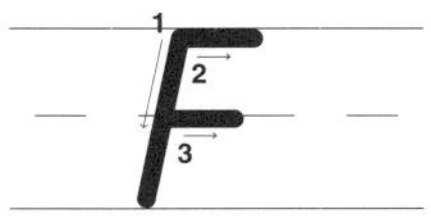

F

(1) Drop.
(2) Glide right.
(3) Glide right.

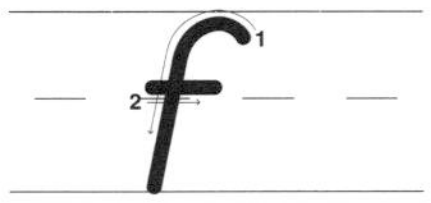

f

(1) Begin at one,
Swing around and
drop low.
(2) Cross.

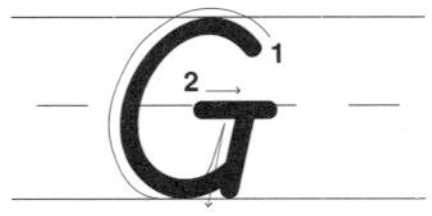

G

(1) Begin at one,
Swing around to three
and drop.
(2) Cross.

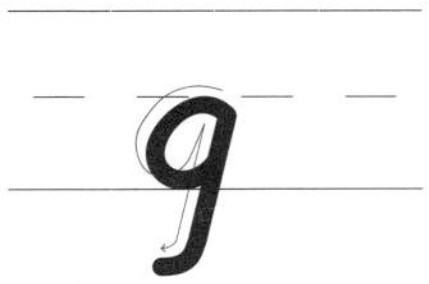

g

Begin at one,
Swing around to lock,
Drop low and hook.

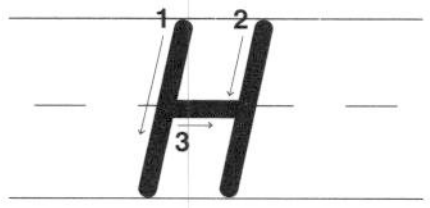

H

(1) Drop.
(2) Drop.
(3) Cross.

h

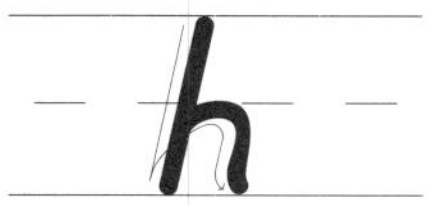

Drop,
Retrace and swing
right,
Drop and curve.

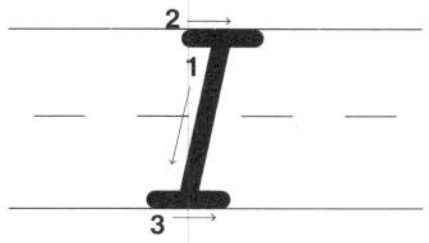

I

(1) Drop.
(2) Cross.
(3) Cross.

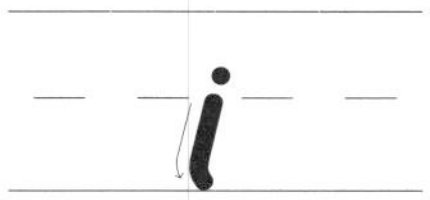

i

Drop and curve.
Dot.

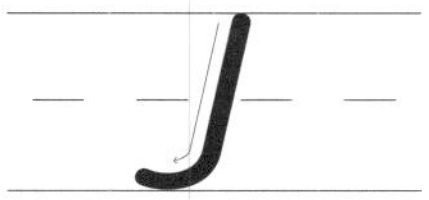

J

Drop and hook.

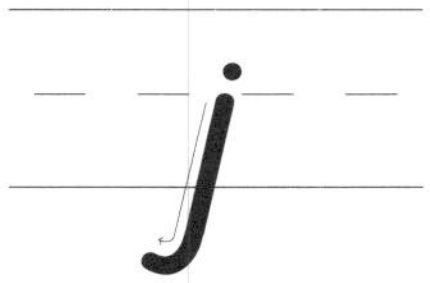

j

Drop low and hook.
Dot.

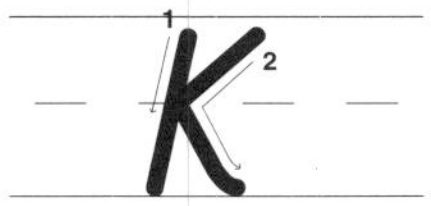

K

(1) Drop.
(2) Drop left,
Then right and curve.

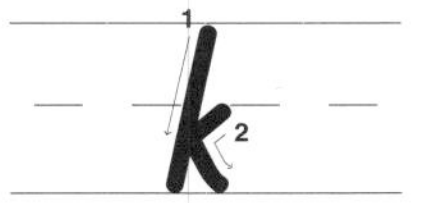

k

(1) Drop.
(2) Drop left,
Then right and curve.

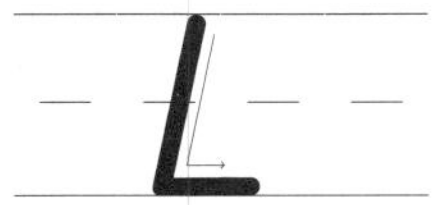

L

Drop.
Glide right.

l

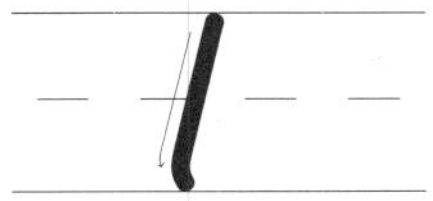

Drop and curve.

M	Drop, retrace and swing right, Drop, retrace and swing right, Drop and curve.
m	Drop, retrace and swing right, Drop, retrace and swing right, Drop and curve.
N	Drop, retrace and swing right, Drop and curve.
n	Drop, retrace and swing right, Drop and curve.
O	Begin at one, Swing around to lock.
o	Begin at one, Swing around to lock.
P	Drop, Retrace and swing around to lock.
p	Drop low, Retrace and swing around to lock.
Q	(1) Begin at one, Swing around to lock. (2) Slash and curve.
q	Begin at one, Swing around to lock, Drop low and crook.

R	Drop, Retrace and swing around to lock, Drop right and curve.
r	Drop, Retrace and swing right.
S	Begin at one, Swerve around and back, Stop at seven.
s	Begin at one, Swerve around and back, Stop at seven.
T	(1) Drop. (2) Cross.
t	(1) Drop and curve. (2) Cross.
U	Drop and swing up, Retrace and curve.
u	Drop and swing up, Retrace and curve.
V	Drop right, Climb right.
v	Drop right, Climb right.

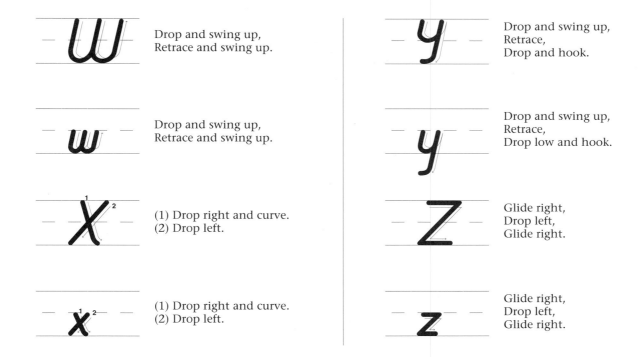

w	Drop and swing up, Retrace and swing up.
w	Drop and swing up, Retrace and swing up.
x	(1) Drop right and curve. (2) Drop left.
x	(1) Drop right and curve. (2) Drop left.
y	Drop and swing up, Retrace, Drop and hook.
y	Drop and swing up, Retrace, Drop low and hook.
Z	Glide right, Drop left, Glide right.
z	Glide right, Drop left, Glide right.

Cursive Stroke Descriptions

Stroke formations

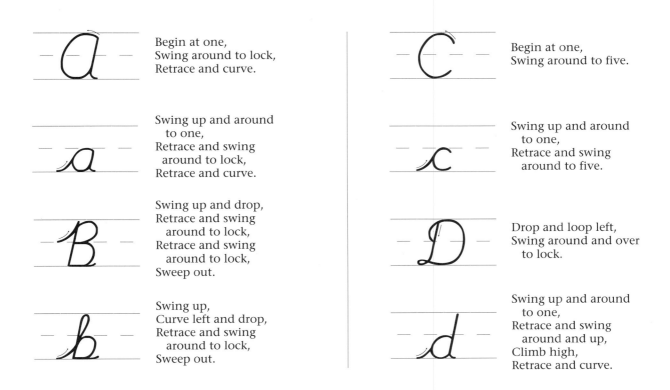

a	Begin at one, Swing around to lock, Retrace and curve.

a	Swing up and around
	    to one,
	Retrace and swing
	    around to lock,
	Retrace and curve.

B	Swing up and drop,
	Retrace and swing
	    around to lock,
	Retrace and swing
	    around to lock,
	Sweep out.

b	Swing up, Curve left and drop, Retrace and swing around to lock, Sweep out.
C	Begin at one, Swing around to five.

c	Swing up and around
	    to one,
	Retrace and swing
	    around to five.

D	Drop and loop left, Swing around and over to lock.

d	Swing up and around
	    to one,
	Retrace and swing
	    around and up,
	Climb high,
	Retrace and curve.

_E_

Begin at one,
Swing around toward
    three,
Swing around to five.

_e_

Swing up toward one
    and around to five.

_F_

(1) Swing over and up,
    Drop and swing left.
(2) Cross.

_f_

Swing up,
Curve left and drop low,
Curve right and up to lock,
Bounce.

_G_

Begin at one,
Swing around to three,
Drop low and loop.

_g_

Swing up and around
    to one,
Retrace and swing
    around to lock,
Drop low and loop.

_H_

(1) Swing up and drop.
(2) Drop and climb left,
    Then glide right.

_h_

Swing up,
Curve left and drop,
Retrace and swing right,
Drop and curve.

_I_

Swing around and up,
Drop and swing left,
Retrace and sweep up.

_i_

Swing up,
Drop and curve.
Dot.

_J_

Swing around and up,
Drop low and loop.

_j_

Swing up,
Drop low and loop.
Dot.

_K_

(1) Swing up and drop.
(2) Drop left,
    Then right and curve.

_k_

Swing up,
Curve left and drop,
Retrace and swing
    around to lock,
Drop right to curve.

_L_

Swing up,
Curve left and drop,
Loop left and sweep across.

_l_

Swing up,
Curve left and loop.

_M_

Swing up,
Drop, retrace and swing
    right,
Drop, retrace and swing
    right,
Drop and curve.

_m_

Swing up,
Drop, retrace and swing
    right,
Drop, retrace and swing
    right,
Drop and curve.

_N_

Swing up,
Drop, retrace and swing
    right,
Drop and curve.

_n_

Swing up,
Drop, retrace and swing
    right,
Drop and curve.

O	Begin at one, Swing around to lock and curl.
o	Swing up and around to one, Retrace and swing around to lock, Sweep out.
P	Swing up and drop, Retrace and swing around to lock.
p	Swing up, Drop low, Retrace and swing around to lock, Sweep out.
Q	(1) Begin at one, Swing around to lock. (2) Curve and slash.
q	Swing up and around to one, Retrace and swing around to lock, Drop low, Curve right and up to lock, Bounce.
R	Swing up and drop, Retrace and swing around to lock, Drop right and curve.
r	Swing up, Slide right, Drop and curve.
S	Swing up, Curve left and loop, Swing around to lock, Sweep out.
s	Swing up, Then down and around to lock, Sweep out.

T	Swing over and up, Drop and swing left.
t	(1) Swing up, Retrace and curve. (2) Cross.
U	Swing up, Drop and swing up, Retrace and curve.
u	Swing up, Drop and swing up, Retrace and curve.
V	Swing up, Drop right, Climb right.
v	Swing up, Drop right, Climb right, Sweep out.
W	Swing up, Drop and swing up, Retrace and swing up.
w	Swing up, Drop and swing up, Retrace and swing up, Sweep out.
X	(1) Swing up, Drop right and curve. (2) Drop left.
x	(1) Swing up, Drop right and curve. (2) Drop left.

Swing up,
Drop and swing up,
Retrace,
Drop low and loop.

Swing up,
Drop and swing up,
Retrace,
Drop low and loop.

Swing up,
Curve around and down
  to six,
Drop low and loop.

Swing up,
Curve around and
  down to six,
Drop low and loop.

Numerical Stroke Descriptions

Stroke formations

0 Begin at one,
Swing around to lock.

1 Drop.

2 Begin at eleven,
Swing right and down
  to the left,
Glide right.

3 Begin at eleven,
Swing around toward nine,
Swing around to seven.

4 (1) Drop and glide right.
(2) Drop.

5 (1) Drop and swing
        around to seven.
(2) Glide right.

6 Swing down and around
  to lock.

7 Glide right,
Drop left.

8 Begin at one,
Swerve around and back,
Then up and around to lock.

9 Begin at one,
Swing around to lock,
Drop.

Student Instructional Materials

Student worktext

HANDWRITING 6 for Christian Schools is a consumable four-color text containing a variety of activities centered on the theme "People and Professions." As students investigate various careers, they learn interesting and pertinent facts about the work that people do. Each writing activity is designed to motivate the young writer as it provides good cursive models for him.

Writing instruments

The most desirable writing tool for the beginning writer is a standard pencil or pen.

Pencil   The pencil should be soft enough to mark readily and long enough to extend past the first knuckle of the hand. Students should learn to care properly for their pencils by keeping them sharp enough to write clearly. Avoid inexpensive pencils that break easily.

Pen   Pens should be of good quality for smooth writing and prevention of smudging. Medium ballpoint pens, similar to pencils in size, will smooth the transition.

Chisel-point pen   A chisel-point pen is needed for the calligraphy lessons. During the first part of the year when only one calligraphy lesson is included in each unit, you will want to distribute and collect the pens for each lesson. At the end of the year when the children do several weeks of consecutive calligraphy lessons, you may want them to keep the pens at their desks.

Handwriting paper

From the *K5 BEGINNINGS* program through grade 2, handwriting paper with half-inch lines is used for all handwriting activities. In grades 3 through 6, handwriting paper with three-eighths-inch lines is used for all writing activities.

Three-eighths-inch ruled notebook paper may be used for handwriting practice. Before permitting your students to use notebook paper that does not have a midline or descender line, establish the following guidelines.

1. Point out the margin lines and instruct students to stay within them.
2. Designate a specific line for name, date, and subject. (See the following example.)

 Do not let sixth graders use college-ruled notebook paper. You can purchase three-eighths-inch-ruled notebook paper or you can reproduce the lines on Appendix page A7.

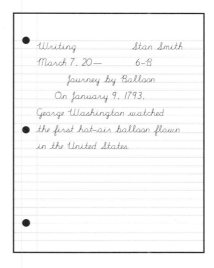

Teacher Instructional Materials

Teacher's manual

HANDWRITING 6 for Christian Schools Teacher's Edition provides the foundation from which all the activities and lesson plans originate. The lessons contain a reduced copy of the student worktext.

Alphabet chart

The cursive alphabet chart is an essential component of the program. It should be displayed in front of the classroom so that students can frequently refer to it.

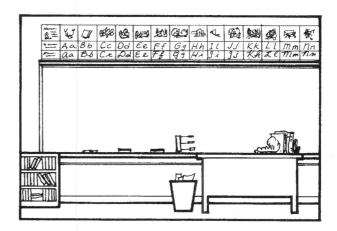

Tools for drawing chalkboard lines

A staff liner holding three (instead of five) pieces of chalk in the top, middle, and bottom clips may be used for drawing handwriting lines on the chalkboard. For a steadier line, a yardstick may be used. Some teachers prefer to set aside a chalkboard or white board and mark permanent lines on it with a felt-tip pen.

Teaching Handwriting

Teacher attitudes

As you teach handwriting, your own handwriting provides a model for your students. Your handwriting must reinforce what you teach. Whether you make charts, write on the chalkboard, or compose personal notes to the students, you should write in the PreCursive or cursive writing style. Your attitude of working to improve your own handwriting will make your students more willing to work to develop theirs.

Letter to parents

The letter to parents that explains the rationale for the handwriting program and a copy of the cursive alphabet are found in the Appendix. Both should be reproduced and distributed to parents.

Scheduling

The prime time for teaching handwriting is in the morning. In grades 1 and 2, a twenty- to thirty-minute period each day is desirable. In grades 3 through 6, instruction in handwriting should be scheduled at least three days a week for a period of twenty minutes.

Biblical principles

Along with the entire *HANDWRITING* series, this worktext aims not only to teach the basic handwriting skills but also to develop Christian attitudes and values. Throughout the lesson plans we have included Bible Action Truths (BATs), the principles of salvation and Christian living that are introduced and taught in the *BIBLE TRUTHS for Christian Schools* curriculum published by Bob Jones University Press. In the lesson plans, these truths are referred to in parentheses by name and number (e.g., BAT: 2e Work). See pages xviii-xx for a list of the Bible Action Truths.

Writing activities

In *HANDWRITING 6 for Christian Schools,* the lessons are designed to reinforce concepts taught in Heritage Studies, science, writing and composition, and Bible.

The worktext pages are perforated so that the assessment pages can be easily removed and graded. The worktext pages with cursive models may be saved and used again.

The optional activity found at the end of each lesson provides additional practice for students. Some activities strengthen small motor skills. Many of the optional activities are to be written on the chalkboard or chart paper. In order to conserve time, you may want to write the suggested verses, poems, quotations, and so forth on chart paper and reuse them.

The Bible for the Moslems

name _____

Many Arabians believe in the teachings of Mohammed. They follow the Koran, a book written by Mohammed. For many years the Koran was not translated into any other languages. Moslems believe that the Koran is God's word only when written in Arabic. In 1865 the Bible was translated into Arabic so that Moslems could read the true Word of God for themselves.

"But though we, or an angel from heaven, preach any other gospel unto you than that which we have preached unto you, let him be accursed." Galatians 1:8

Write the verse.

Use with Lesson 6.   11

New students

HANDWRITING 6 provides a review of cursive letters taught in earlier grades. Most new students quickly learn the new letter forms.

New students or students who have poor writing skills may benefit from learning the PreCursive letters since they provide a good foundation for the cursive letters.

Students who have been previously taught another handwriting style and have good handwriting skills should not be required to learn the new letter forms.

Seating arrangements

For any instruction in handwriting, seating arrangements should make the best use of lighting so that students have no shadows on their papers. Overhead lighting should fill in most shadows and provide even illumination in all parts of the room. In addition, natural light should come at such an angle that a student's writing hand does not cast shadows on his paper. Thus, for the right-handed student, natural light should come over his left shoulder; for the left-handed student, it should come over his right shoulder.

If you seat students by groups to make the best use of lighting, you will notice other advantages as well. Seating left-handed students together prevents writing-arm collision. In addition, when you give special instructions to left-handed students, you can give them to all left-handed students at once.

Desk position and posture

Good posture affects handwriting. Each child should sit comfortably in his chair with his feet on the floor. The desk should be slightly higher than the student's waist. The student should sit, not leaning to the left or to the right, but bending slightly forward. His forearms should rest on his desk.

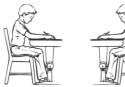

Paper position

The position of the paper is related to the child's posture. Each student should place his paper directly in front of his eyes and under his writing hand. The nonwriting hand lies on the paper to hold it still. The slant of the paper will allow him to see around his hand as he works; thus he will not have to lean to the left or right to see his work. A right-handed student will tilt his paper to the left so that it lies parallel to his writing arm. The left-handed student will tilt his paper to the right 30 to 45 degrees. These paper positions will eliminate the hooked-hand position which restricts hand and finger movement needed for writing. The hooked-hand position must also be avoided to prevent poor posture.

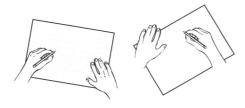

Pencil / Pen hold

In the accepted position for pencil and pen hold, the thumb and the index finger grasp the writing instrument, letting it rest on the middle finger. The last two fingers arch under the middle finger to support it. The hand rests on its side. The student should hold the writing instrument about one inch from the writing point. The writing instrument will point toward the shoulder. A student should hold his pencil or pen lightly enough so that you can pull it out of his hand with little resistance. In general, low or medium pressure produces better writing. Improving and/or maintaining correct pencil and pen hold is one of your greatest responsibilities as a handwriting teacher. It is very difficult and often impossible to try to correct an improper pencil hold that is an established habit.

Writing at the chalkboard

Writing at the chalkboard provides the student the opportunity to practice letter formations under the watchful eye of the teacher. The activity also allows for the development of muscles which are used in the writing process.

The following guidelines should be followed to make chalkboard writing a meaningful activity.

1. The student should stand comfortably about an arm's length from the chalkboard, allowing room for the elbow to bend at the proper angle (down and away from the body). Both feet should be on the floor.
2. All writing should be done at the student's eye level.
3. The chalk should be held between the thumb and the first two fingers. It should be long enough to be held easily.
4. The writing should be done with light, sweeping strokes, with the end of the chalk rounded so that it will not squeak.

Special handwriting problems

Illegible handwriting is often a clue to both you and the parents that a child may have special learning problems. Some children cannot write well because they are not mature enough to acquire the motor skills that are necessary to form letters and words. Other children may have poor vision, a problem that a visit to an optometrist will often solve. A small number of children have a specific learning disability which makes it difficult for them to remember the large amount of information they are exposed to each day. Students with learning problems should be referred to a learning specialist for evaluation and diagnosis.

Letter Formation

Students can easily master letter formations if you follow the procedure listed below.

1. Verbalize the letter formation as you write each new letter on the chalkboard. If a letter has more than one stroke, use a different color of chalk for each stroke.

2. Tell students to stand and air-trace the letter with you as you verbalize the letter formation again.

3. Direct students in small groups to write the letter on the chalkboard as you verbalize the letter formation once more.

4. Guide activities on the worktext page. Tell students to note the arrow that indicates the stroke direction, finger-trace the black letter, and then pencil-trace the gray letters.

5. Circulate among the students as they practice the new letters. Make sure that they are writing each letter correctly. Evaluation of the finished letters may not reveal incorrect stroke direction; however, when students increase their writing speed, these incorrect strokes will lead to illegible writing.

Letter alignment

Uneven or illegible writing is often the result of letters that do not rest on the base line. Improper letter height can also produce an uneven top alignment. The simplicity of letter forms used in this series helps each student maintain proper letter alignment. Most letters are given a specific starting point related to one of several guidelines.

top line ————————————————

base line ————————————————

Slant of letters

One of the major causes of illegibility is irregular letter slant. Students often experience their greatest difficulty with slant during the transition to cursive writing. The PreCursive alphabet avoids this transition problem by presenting slanted letters from the beginning. Although an approximate slant of 5 to 15 degrees is suggested, the emphasis should always be on consistency without extremes. If necessary, left-handed writers may write vertically or slightly backhanded as long as the slant is consistent.

Spacing

Even spacing between letters and words is essential to legible writing. Carefully designed worktext activities guide each student in developing the correct spacing.

Students need to know how to leave margins and how to correctly place their writing on the paper. The special forms needed for writing correspondence, taking notes, and composing poetry are all part of the handwriting instruction given in *HANDWRITING 6 for Christian Schools*.

Neatness

Neatness also contributes to legibility. You may want to teach the children to eliminate undesirable handwriting by drawing one line through it rather than scribbling over or erasing it. Sometimes their vigorous erasing eliminates both the writing and the paper. Of course, learning to erase small mistakes properly comes from instruction in handwriting also. Teach students to think about what they are writing to avoid careless errors, but be realistic about the degree of neatness you expect from them.

Rhythm

Rhythm is the regularity of pressure patterns of fingers on the writing instrument. When we write, we tend to put more pressure on the instrument as we draw the line down toward us and less pressure as we push it up and away. Because of the simple one-stroke letters, students begin to learn rhythm from the outset of instruction in PreCursive. It will become a part of the student's writing when he begins to see whole words, when he attains a speed that is appropriate for his skill, and when he eliminates unnecessary tension from his pencil hold and small-muscle movements. Students need to attain consistency of rhythm before they work to increase their speed.

Evaluation of Handwriting

Student evaluation

In order to be most effective, the evaluation of handwriting should directly involve the student. *HANDWRITING 6 for Christian Schools* recognizes the importance of teaching the students to evaluate their own progress.

A classroom checklist that is displayed where it can be seen at all times will help each student correct errors in his writing as they occur. It should include the following questions.

1. Do I hold my pencil/pen correctly?
2. Do I have good posture?
3. Are all my letters resting on the base line?
4. Do all small letters touch the midline, and do all tall letters touch the top line?
5. Are the spaces between the letters and words even?
6. Do all my letters slant the same way?
7. Are all my downstrokes parallel?
8. Are all my letters with loops well formed?
9. Are all closed letters formed correctly?

By comparing past and present work, the students can be encouraged to improve their handwriting. The work can be kept in a writing folder, and individual assignments for writing practice can be made from the papers. If this comparison is made on a regular basis, it will keep the students' attention centered on improvement and will help to positively motivate them.

Teacher evaluation

The evaluation form found in the Appendix is designed for your use when you evaluate each student's handwriting. It also provides space for helpful suggestions to students and parents as to how handwriting skills can be improved.

A pretest is included in the worktext. It is to help you note the letters that are going to require the most attention. It also provides a basis for information to help each student see his progress. This page should not be graded or sent home.

The assessment pages included throughout the book should indicate progress made by the student. These pages, when compared by the students to pretests and past assessments, will show them their success and encourage them to continue improving. These pages may be graded, but should be kept for evaluating progress during the entire year. The evaluation form in the Appendix may be a helpful guide. A post-test is included following the completion of the worktext. Comparing the pretest and post-test should give you an accurate picture of the students' learning.

Developing Handwriting Consciousness

Displaying students' handwriting

Students' work should be displayed whenever possible, omitting no student in this effective method of approval. Several bulletin-board displays are included in the Appendix. Used throughout the year, they will instill a sense of pride in each student, encouraging him to improve his handwriting and to do it heartily as unto the Lord.

Other classroom activities using handwriting

When the students do other activities that use writing, have them use the same lined paper or lines of the same size as those used for handwriting activities. To label maps and drawings or other projects, cut out pieces of lined paper and glue them down. For all activities involving handwriting, consider the length of the activity. Choose assignments that your students can write comfortably in a reasonable amount of time. Even though the primary goal of an activity may be something other than good handwriting, students must understand that all writing contributes to writing habits. However, when students are asked to write original material such as stories or letters, handwriting evaluation should not be made on the brainstorming process. Students should be allowed to recopy their original work if an assessment is desired.

Student Objectives

Given the proper instruction, the students will be able to do the following:

Demonstrate good posture, correct paper position, and a proper tension-free pencil hold.

Relate the cursive letter to its PreCursive counterpart.

Use vocabulary that describes letter spacing: space, dashes, indentation, margin.

Use vocabulary that describes letter alignment: top line, midline, base line.

Gain skill in reading cursive writing.

Master the correct order and direction of strokes for each cursive letter and numeral.

Practice and use the cursive joining strokes.

Use adequate spacing between cursive letters, words, and sentences.

Write legibly, incorporating neatness, consistent slant and spacing, and correct alignment.

Develop a concern for readability and neatness.

Develop a rhythm and increase writing speed within ability limits.

Write letters the correct size: with a middle guideline and without a middle guideline.

Arrange words neatly on paper by centering titles, indenting paragraphs, and keeping within acceptable margins.

Bible Action Truths

The quality and consistency of a man's decisions determine his character. Christian character is developed by consistently making godly decisions. It is within this framework that lasting peace and happiness are found.

Too often Christians live by only vague guidance—for instance, that we should "do good" to all men. While doing good is desirable, more specific guidance will lead to more consistent decisions.

Consistent decisions are made when man acts on Bible principles—or Bible Action Truths. The thirty-seven Bible Action Truths (listed under eight general principles) provide Christians with specific goals for their actions and attitudes. Study the Scriptures indicated for a fuller understanding of the principles and the Bible Action Truths.

Thousands have found this format helpful in identifying and applying principles of behavior. Yet there is no "magic" in this formula. As you study the Word of God, you likely will find other truths that speak to you. The key is for you to study the Scriptures, look for Bible Action Truths, and be sensitive to the leading of the Holy Spirit.

1. **SALVATION–SEPARATION PRINCIPLE**
   Salvation results from God's direct action. Although man is unable to work for this "gift of God," the Christian's reaction to salvation should be to separate himself from the world unto God.

   a. **Understanding Jesus Christ** (Matthew 3:17; 16:16; I Corinthians 15:3-4; Philippians 2:9-11) Jesus is the Son of God. He was sent to earth to die on the cross for our sins. He was buried but rose from the dead after three days.

   b. **Repentance and faith** (Luke 13:3; Isaiah 55:7; Acts 5:30-31; Hebrews 11:6; Acts 16:31) If we believe that Jesus died for our sins, we can accept Him as our Savior. We must be sorry for our sins, turn from them, confess them to God, and believe that He will forgive us.

   c. **Separation from the world** (John 17:6, 11, 14, 18; II Corinthians 6:14-18; I John 2:15-16; James 4:4; Romans 16:17-18; II John 10-11) After we are saved, we should live a different life. We should try to be like Christ and not live like those who are unsaved.

2. **SONSHIP–SERVANT PRINCIPLE**
   Only by an act of God the Father could sinful man become a son of God. As a son of God, however, the Christian must realize that he has been "bought with a price"; he is now Christ's servant.

   a. **Authority** (Romans 13:1-7; I Peter 2:13-19; I Timothy 6:1-5; Hebrews 13:17; Matthew 22:21; I Thessalonians 5:12-13) We should respect, honor, and obey those in authority over us.

   b. **Servanthood** (Philippians 2:7-8; Ephesians 6:5-8) Just as Christ was a humble servant while He was on earth, we should also be humble and obedient.

   c. **Faithfulness** (I Corinthians 4:2; Matthew 25:23; Luke 9:62) We should do our work so that God and others can depend on us.

   d. **Goal setting** (Proverbs 13:12, 19; Philippians 3:13; Colossians 3:2; I Corinthians 9:24) To be a faithful servant means that we must set goals for our work. We should look forward to finishing a job and going on to something more.

   e. **Work** (Ephesians 4:28; II Thessalonians 3:10-12) God does not honor a lazy servant. He wants us to be busy and dependable workers.

   f. **Enthusiasm** (Colossians 3:23; Romans 12:11) We should do all tasks with energy and with a happy, willing spirit.

3. **UNIQUENESS–UNITY PRINCIPLE**
   No one is a mere person; God has created each individual a unique being. But because God has an overall plan for His creation, each unique member must contribute to the unity of the entire body.

   a. **Self-concept** (Psalms 8:3-8; 139; II Corinthians 5:17; Ephesians 2:10; 4:1-3, 11-13; II Peter 1:10) We are special creatures in God's plan. He has given each of us special abilities to use in our lives for Him.

   b. **Mind** (Philippians 2:5; 4:8; II Corinthians 10:5; Proverbs 4:23; 23:7; Luke 6:45; Romans 7:23, 25; Daniel 1:8; James 1:8) We should give our thoughts and minds to God. What we do and say really begins in our minds. We should try to think of ourselves humbly as Christ did when He lived on earth.

   c. **Emotional control** (Galatians 5:24; Proverbs 16:32; 25:28; II Timothy 1:7; Acts 20:24) With the help of God and the power of the Holy Spirit, we should have control over our feelings. We must be careful not to act out of anger.

   d. **Body as a temple** (I Corinthians 3:16-17; 6:19-20) We should remember that our bodies are the dwelling place of God's Holy Spirit. We should keep ourselves pure, honest, and dedicated to God's will.

   e. **Unity of Christ and the church** (John 17:21; Ephesians 2:19-22; 5:23-32; II Thessalonians 3:6, 14-15) Since we are saved, we are now part of God's family and should unite ourselves with others to worship and grow as Christians. Christ is the head of His church, which includes all believers, and He wants us to work together as His church in carrying out His plans, but He forbids us to work in fellowship with disobedient brethren.

4. **HOLINESS–HABIT PRINCIPLE**

Believers are declared holy as a result of Christ's finished action on the cross. Daily holiness of life, however, comes from forming godly habits. A Christian must consciously establish godly patterns of action; he must develop habits of holiness.

   a. **Sowing and reaping** (Galatians 6:7-8; Hosea 8:7; Matthew 6:1-8) We must remember that we will be rewarded according to the kind of work we have done. If we are faithful, we will be rewarded. If we are unfaithful, we will not be rewarded. We cannot fool God.

   b. **Purity** (I Thessalonians 4:1-7; I Peter 1:22) We should try to live lives that are free from sin. We should keep our minds, words, and deeds clean and pure.

   c. **Honesty** (II Corinthians 8:21; Romans 12:17; Proverbs 16:8; Ephesians 4:25) We should not lie. We should be honest in every way. Even if we could gain more by being dishonest, we should still be honest. God can see all things.

   d. **Victory** (I Corinthians 10:13; Romans 8:37; I John 5:4; John 16:33; I Corinthians 15:57-58) If we constantly try to be pure, honest, and Christlike, with God's help we will be able to overcome temptations.

5. **LOVE–LIFE PRINCIPLE**

We love God because He first loved us. God's action of manifesting His love to us through His Son demonstrates the truth that love must be exercised. Since God acted in love toward us, believers must act likewise by showing godly love to others.

   a. **Love** (I John 3:11, 16-18; 4:7-21; Ephesians 5:2; I Corinthians 13; John 15:17) God's love to us is the greatest love possible. We should, in turn, show our love for others by our words and actions.

   b. **Giving** (II Corinthians 9:6-8; Proverbs 3:9-10; Luke 6:38) We should give cheerfully to God the first part of all we earn. We should also give to others unselfishly.

   c. **Evangelism and missions** (Psalm 126:5-6; Matthew 28:18-20; Romans 1:16-17; II Corinthians 5:11-21) We should be busy telling others about the love of God and His plan of salvation. We should share in the work of foreign missionaries by our giving and prayers.

   d. **Communication** (Ephesians 4:22-29; Colossians 4:6; James 3:2-13; Isaiah 50:4) We should have control of our tongues so that we will not say things displeasing to God. We should encourage others and be kind and helpful in what we say.

   e. **Friendliness** (Psalm 19:63; Proverbs 18:24; 17:17) We should be friendly to others, and we should be loyal to those who love and serve God.

6. **COMMUNION–CONSECRATION PRINCIPLE**

Because sin separates man from God, any communion between man and God must be achieved by God's direct action of removing sin. Once communion is established, the believer's reaction should be to maintain a consciousness of this fellowship by living a consecrated life.

   a. **Bible study** (I Peter 2:2-3; II Timothy 2:15; Psalm 119) To grow as Christians, we must spend time with God daily by reading His Word.

   b. **Prayer** (I Chronicles 16:11; I Thessalonians 5:17; John 15:7, 16; 16:24; Psalm 145:18; Romans 8:26-27) We should bring all our requests to God, trusting Him to answer them in His own way.

   c. **Spirit-filled** (Romans 8:13-14; Galatians 5:16, 22-23; Ephesians 5:8-19; I John 1:7-9) We should let the Holy Spirit rule in our hearts and show us what to say and do. We should not say and do just what we want to, for those things are often wrong and harmful to others.

   d. **Clear conscience** (I Timothy 1:19; Acts 24:16) To be good Christians, we cannot have wrong acts or thoughts or words bothering our consciences. We must confess them to God and to those people against whom we have sinned. We cannot live lives close to God if we have guilty consciences.

   e. **Forgiveness** (Ephesians 4:30-32; Luke 17:3-4; Colossians 3:13; Matthew 18:15-17; Mark 11:25-26) We must ask forgiveness of God when we have done wrong. Just as God forgives our sins freely, we should forgive others when they do wrong things to us.

7. **GRACE–GRATITUDE PRINCIPLE**

Grace is unmerited favor. Man does not deserve God's grace. However, after God bestows His grace, believers should react with an overflow of gratitude.

   a. **Grace** (I Corinthians 15:10; Ephesians 2:8-9) Without God's grace we would be sinners on our way to hell. He loved us when we did not deserve His love and provided for us a way to escape sin's punishment by the death of His Son on the cross.

   b. **Exaltation of Christ** (Colossians 1:12-21; Ephesians 1:17-23; Philippians 2:9-11; Galatians 6:14; Hebrews 1:2-3; John 1:1-4, 14; 5:23) We should realize and remember at all times the power, holiness, majesty, and perfection of Christ, and we should give Him the praise and glory for everything that is accomplished through us.

c. **Praise** (Psalm 107:8; Hebrews 13:15; I Peter 2:9; Ephesians 1:6; I Chronicles 16:23-26; 29:11-13) Remembering God's great love and goodness toward us, we should continually praise His name.

d. **Contentment** (Philippians 4:11; I Timothy 6:6-8; Psalm 77:3; Proverbs 15:16; Hebrews 13:5) Money, houses, cars, and all things on earth will last only for a little while. God has given us just what He meant for us to have. We should be happy and content with what we have, knowing that God will provide for us all that we need. We should also be happy wherever God places us.

e. **Humility** (I Peter 5:5-6; Philippians 2:3-4) We should not be proud and boastful but should be willing to be quiet and in the background. Our reward will come from God on Judgment Day, and men's praise to us here on earth will not matter at all. Christ was humble when He lived on earth, and we should be like Him.

8. **POWER—PREVAILING PRINCIPLE**

Believers can prevail only as God gives the power. "I can do all things through Christ" (Philippians 4:13). God is the source of our power used in fighting the good fight of faith.

a. **Faith in God's promises** (II Peter 1:4; Philippians 4:6; Romans 4:16-21; I Thessalonians 5:18; Romans 8:28; I Peter 5:7; Hebrews 3:18–4:11) God always remains true to His promises. Believing that He will keep all the promises in His Word, we should be determined fighters for Him.

b. **Faith in the power of the Word of God** (Hebrews 4:12; Jeremiah 23:29; Psalm 119; I Peter 1:23-25) God's Word is powerful and endures forever. All other things will pass away, but God's Word shall never pass away because it is written to us from God, and God is eternal.

c. **Fight** (Ephesians 6:11-17; II Timothy 4:7-8; I Timothy 6:12; I Peter 5:8-9) God does not have any use for lazy or cowardly fighters. We must work and fight against sin, using the Word of God as our weapon against the devil. What we do for God now will determine how much He will reward us in heaven.

d. **Courage** (I Chronicles 28:20; Joshua 1:9; Hebrews 13:6; Ephesians 3:11-12; Acts 4:13, 31) God has promised us that He will not forsake us; therefore, we should not be afraid to speak out against sin. We should remember that we are armed with God's strength.

Calligraphy Introduction

Major Goals

To provide a motivational tool.

To re-create interest in good handwriting.

To introduce an alternate style of handwriting.

Historical Background

The study of ancient writing, paleography, is concerned both with inscription and calligraphy. Inscription is script on stone, bone, metal, or other hard surfaces; calligraphy is script on perishable materials such as papyrus, parchment, textiles, or paper. But calligraphy is more than just script on perishable materials; it is—as the Greek word implies—the art of fine handwriting. And the term *calligraphy* applies to letters, words, pages, or even whole documents to which artistic principles and skilled penmanship have been applied.

In this handwriting program, you will have an opportunity to introduce the students to one style of calligraphy—Chancery cursive. Chancery cursive, sometimes called Chancery italic, was developed by scribes working in chanceries (offices) under the jurisdiction of bishops. The popularity of the style grew during the late fifteenth and early sixteenth centuries until many artists, nobles, and scholars of the Italian Renaissance used it. In 1522, the scribe Lodovico degli Arrighi made this style available to the public when he published the first writing manual ever produced.

Calligraphy Letter Stroke Descriptions

(1) Drop left and glide left.
(2) Swing left and glide right,
  Drop and glide right.
(3) Cross.

(1) Drop and slight curve left.
(2) Swing left and up,
  Glide right, around, and down to lock,
  Retrace, around, and down to lock.

Glide left,
Swing around to lock,
Retrace and curve.

Glide left,
Drop,
Retrace and swing around to lock.

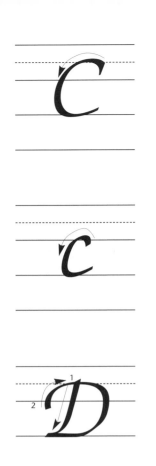

Glide left,
Swing around.

Curve up,
Swing around.

(1) Drop and slight curve left.
(2) Swing left and up, Glide right, around, and down to lock,

(1) Glide left, Swing around.
(2) Glide left, Drop to lock and curve.

(1) Drop and curve left, Retrace, glide right and curve up.
(2) Swing left and glide right and curve down.
(3) Cross.

(1) Swing around left.
(2) Swing around right to halfway between base line and body line.

(1) Drop and glide left.
(2) Swing left and glide right and slight curve up.
(3) Cross.

(1) Glide left, Drop low and hook left.
(2) Cross right below the body line.

(1) Glide left, Swing around.
(2) Glide right, Drop low and hook.

(1) Glide left and swing down to base line.
(2) Drop low, Glide left, Swing up right to lock.

(1) Swing left and around, Drop and glide left.
(2) Start high, Glide left, Drop and glide right.
(3) Cross.

Glide left,
Drop,
Retrace and swing right,
Drop and curve.

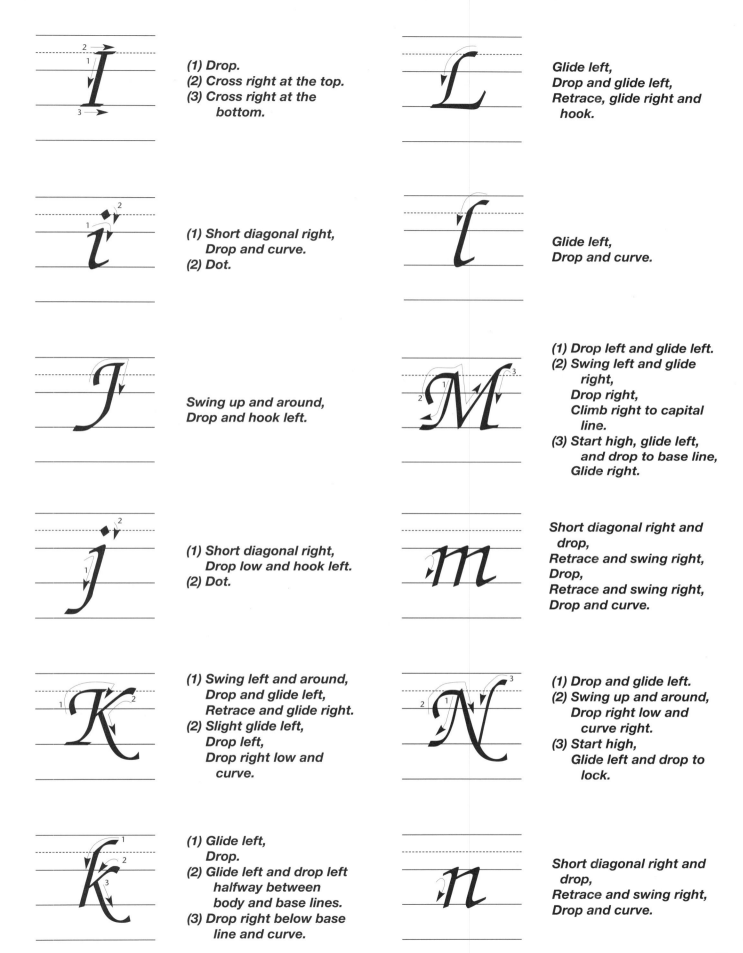

I
(1) Drop.
(2) Cross right at the top.
(3) Cross right at the bottom.

L
Glide left,
Drop and glide left,
Retrace, glide right and hook.

i
(1) Short diagonal right, Drop and curve.
(2) Dot.

l
Glide left,
Drop and curve.

J
Swing up and around,
Drop and hook left.

M
(1) Drop left and glide left.
(2) Swing left and glide right,
Drop right,
Climb right to capital line.
(3) Start high, glide left, and drop to base line,
Glide right.

j
(1) Short diagonal right, Drop low and hook left.
(2) Dot.

m
Short diagonal right and drop,
Retrace and swing right,
Drop,
Retrace and swing right,
Drop and curve.

K
(1) Swing left and around,
Drop and glide left,
Retrace and glide right.
(2) Slight glide left,
Drop left,
Drop right low and curve.

N
(1) Drop and glide left.
(2) Swing up and around,
Drop right low and curve right.
(3) Start high,
Glide left and drop to lock.

k
(1) Glide left,
Drop.
(2) Glide left and drop left halfway between body and base lines.
(3) Drop right below base line and curve.

n
Short diagonal right and drop,
Retrace and swing right,
Drop and curve.

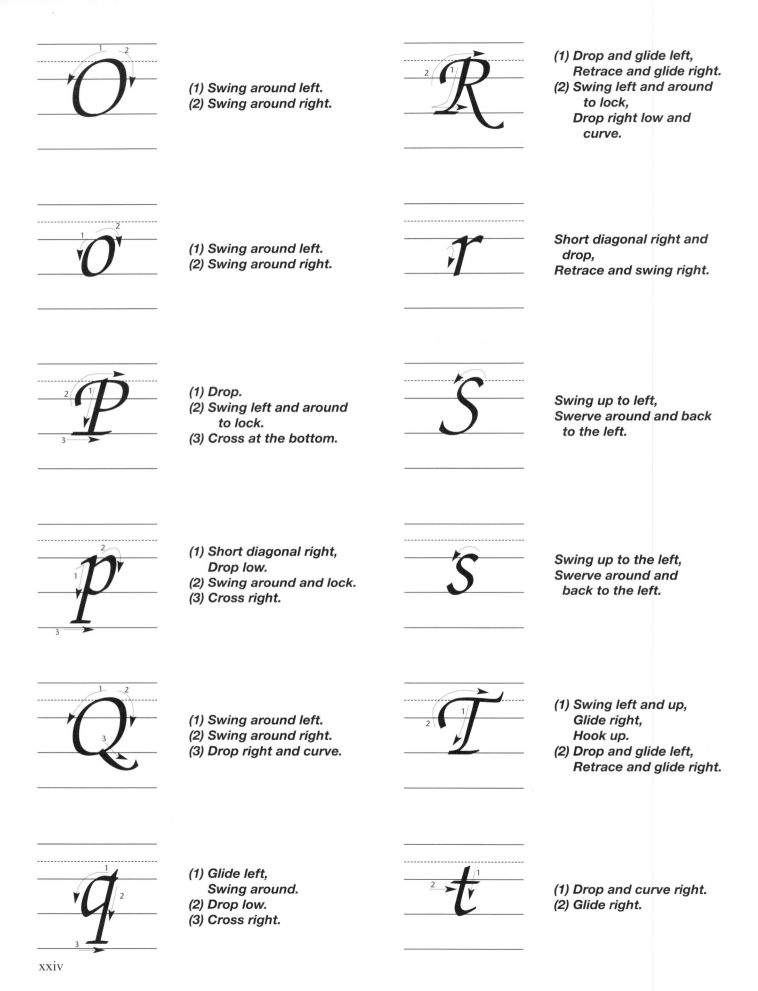

O
(1) Swing around left.
(2) Swing around right.

R
(1) Drop and glide left,
Retrace and glide right.
(2) Swing left and around
to lock,
Drop right low and
curve.

o
(1) Swing around left.
(2) Swing around right.

r
Short diagonal right and
drop,
Retrace and swing right.

P
(1) Drop.
(2) Swing left and around
to lock.
(3) Cross at the bottom.

S
Swing up to left,
Swerve around and back
to the left.

p
(1) Short diagonal right,
Drop low.
(2) Swing around and lock.
(3) Cross right.

s
Swing up to the left,
Swerve around and
back to the left.

Q
(1) Swing around left.
(2) Swing around right.
(3) Drop right and curve.

T
(1) Swing left and up,
Glide right,
Hook up.
(2) Drop and glide left,
Retrace and glide right.

q
(1) Glide left,
Swing around.
(2) Drop low.
(3) Cross right.

t
(1) Drop and curve right.
(2) Glide right.

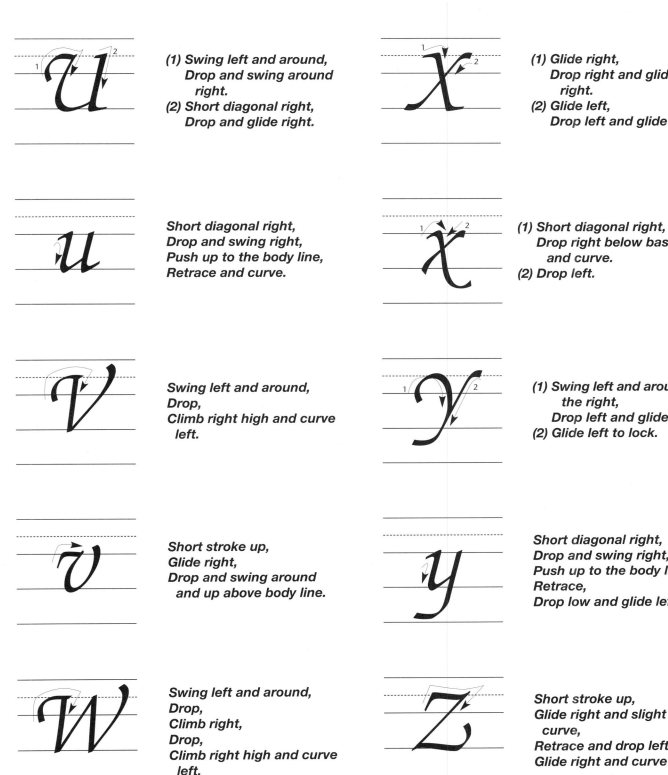

(1) *Swing left and around,*
   Drop and swing around
   right.
(2) *Short diagonal right,*
   Drop and glide right.

(1) *Glide right,*
   Drop right and glide
   right.
(2) *Glide left,*
   Drop left and glide left.

Short diagonal right,
Drop and swing right,
Push up to the body line,
Retrace and curve.

(1) *Short diagonal right,*
   Drop right below base line
   and curve.
(2) *Drop left.*

Swing left and around,
Drop,
Climb right high and curve
   left.

(1) *Swing left and around to*
   the right,
   Drop left and glide left.
(2) *Glide left to lock.*

Short stroke up,
Glide right,
Drop and swing around
   and up above body line.

Short diagonal right,
Drop and swing right,
Push up to the body line,
Retrace,
Drop low and glide left.

Swing left and around,
Drop,
Climb right,
Drop,
Climb right high and curve
   left.

Short stroke up,
Glide right and slight
   curve,
Retrace and drop left,
Glide right and curve up.

Short stroke up,
Glide right,
Drop and swing around
   and up to body line,
Retrace and swing around
   and up above body line.

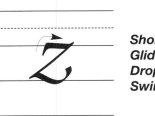

Short stroke up,
Glide right,
Drop left,
Swing right and curve up.

Calligraphy Numeral Stroke Descriptions

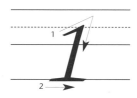

(1) Short diagonal right, Drop.
(2) Cross at bottom.

(1) Swing around to the left.
(2) Swing right and around to lock.

Swing up and around Drop left, Glide right and hook.

Short diagonal left, Glide right, Drop left, Slight curve right.

Swing up and around to the left, Retrace and swing around to the left.

(1) Swing down, Swerve around and back.
(2) Swing left and around to lock.
(3) Swing right and around to lock.

(1) Drop left, Glide right.
(2) Drop.

Swing around left and up and around, Swing down left to the base line.

(1) Drop below body line and swing around.
(2) Glide right and curve up.

Student Instructional Materials

Student worktext

Three sections in the student worktext contain calligraphy activities. First, you will find a lowercase calligraphy lesson at the end of each unit. These lessons introduce calligraphy terms and the stroke descriptions for the lowercase Chancery cursive letters.

Second, the Character Quality unit at the end of the student worktext is a calligraphy unit. The name *Character Quality* was given to this unit because the students will be studying character traits as they practice their calligraphy and because they should strive to write "quality characters" as they practice. This calligraphy unit contains the stroke descriptions for the uppercase Chancery cursive letters and the calligraphy numerals and lessons in spacing and layout in calligraphy. Finally, at the end of the unit several calligraphy reference pages present helpful information to be used throughout the year during calligraphy lessons. The Calligraphy Glossary includes background information and definitions of terms. A set of Calligraphy Tips summarizes all the tips listed on the top of the student calligraphy pages. A variety of sample calligraphy projects is also included to provide examples for the students to follow.

Third, you will find on an insert in the center of each student worktext a set of guide sheets for calligraphy. This insert can be removed by tearing along the perforation, making two guide sheets. Give one guide sheet to each student and store the others in case one gets lost or wears out. Each guide sheet has two sides—the Lowercase Guide Sheet and the Advanced Guide Sheet. As you inspect the Lowercase Guide Sheet, you will notice that it has two of the five guidelines (the body and base lines) and the slant lines. The Advanced Guide Sheet has all five of the guidelines (body, base, capital, ascender, and descender lines) as well as the slant lines.

Writing instruments

For your convenience a felt chisel-point pen is available from Bob Jones University Press. For most sixth-grade students this is the recommended choice. Although this type of pen does not have interchangeable tips, it has the advantage of not needing to be filled constantly with ink. This pen is compatible with the guide sheet designed for this program. Because of the increased interest in calligraphy, however, you will find other types of pens available.

You could, for example, consider a calligraphy fountain pen. Unlike the chisel-point pens, these pens have a variety of interchangeable tips. And like the chisel-point pens, they do not need to be constantly filled with ink. The basic disadvantage of this pen is that the thickness of the barrel may not provide a comfortable grip. You could also consider the use of India ink, a pen nib, and a pen staff. Let us look at each of these items in order.

1. India ink is a very black, opaque ink. (*Note:* Be careful with it because once it is dry, it is permanent.)

2. A C-3 pen nib would be appropriate for an x-height of $3/8$ inches—the x-height of the guide sheet designed for this program. (*Note:* The x-height is the height between the base and body lines on the guide sheet. It is equal to five pen widths.) A pen nib should not be dipped into the ink; it should be filled with the dropper that comes in the ink bottle. When filling a pen nib with a dropper, fill it only about half way up the opening between the gold and the silver parts of the pen nib. When you are finished using the pen, remove the nib from the pen staff, take the nib to the sink, and use a toothbrush to clean it under running water. Pat the nib dry with paper towel once you are done cleaning it. This care will help preserve the life of the pen.

3. There are many pen staffs available, and no one is right for everyone. They come in plastic, wood, and aluminum. Some are thick and some are thin. Some have groove grips for the fingers, some have a band of cork, and some are smooth. What is important is how it feels in your hand. You may need to try several before you are satisfied. In caring for your pen staff, remember not to get the metal inside the staff wet. You should not clean your nib while it is still in the staff.

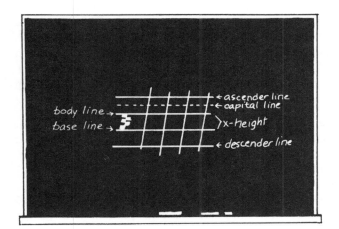

Handwriting paper

Typing paper used over a guide sheet is the paper recommended for the Continued Practice sections in the Calligraphy Lessons. If you have some paper through which you cannot see the guide sheet or if you choose to use a pen size different from the one for the guide sheet, then draw four pencil lines five pen-widths apart on the paper. Put in a capital line halfway between the body and the ascender lines. Erase the lines after the ink is completely dry. Also, you can use any ruled notebook paper where the lines are three-eighths of an inch apart.

Teacher Instructional Materials

Teacher's manual

This teacher's manual can be divided into three sections: the introductions to the regular alphabet and to calligraphy, the lessons, and the Appendix. In teaching calligraphy, this Calligraphy Introduction and the calligraphy lessons will be of invaluable help.

Teaching Calligraphy

The calligraphy lessons included in this program are not designed to teach everything there is to know about calligraphy. It is not our purpose for the lessons to be difficult or to be graded. They are written, however, with the intent of introducing you and the students to calligraphy. The calligraphy lessons should prove to be a motivational factor to spur you and your students on to better handwriting. To ensure success in teaching calligraphy, you should become familiar with the contents of the calligraphy lessons and practice the letters prior to teaching them. In fact, as you become familiar with the design of the book, you may see the need to look ahead to the uppercase calligraphy lessons as you teach the lowercase calligraphy lessons. This may be helpful to you because the uppercase lessons follow one right after the other, and you may not have time to learn them quickly enough. It may also prove helpful to you and the students if you provide a learning center with a pen, book, guide sheet, and typing paper for practice between lessons.

The Calligraphy Tips section at the back of the student worktext contains a summary of the positions you need to cover when teaching calligraphy. These key concepts were included in the worktext so that you could direct the students to those pages when you teach the proper positions. The Calligraphy Tips section covers the proper body position, paper position, and pen hold. Let us cover each of these concepts briefly.

Body position

Direct the students to sit up straight, keep their feet flat on the floor, and keep their bodies facing the desk.

Paper position

Direct the students to line up the bottom of their paper with the horizontal edge of their desk. Direct left-handed students to slant the paper if needed. Tell the students to move the paper to the left as they write across the page. Point out that moving the paper under their hand (and not their hand across the paper) will help them maintain a consistent pen angle.

Pen hold

Direct the students to hold the pen loosely between the thumb and the first and second fingers. Tell them to rest the pen near the first knuckle and hold the pen upright so that it is easier to control.

Order of letter presentation

In this program, the calligraphy letters are presented in groups containing similar stroke patterns. The Chancery cursive lowercase letters are interspersed with the regular cursive lessons, and the Chancery cursive uppercase letters and numerals are presented in a separate Character Quality unit.

Demonstrating stroke descriptions

The overhead projector is recommended for demonstrating stroke descriptions. Use a broad-tipped felt-tip pen. Guide lines appropriate to broad-tipped overhead markers are included in the Appendix. The students may also enjoy demonstrating the strokes on the overhead.

You may choose instead to use a white board. You will need to draw lines five pen widths apart on the white board.

The chalkboard is also an option. You will need to draw lines five chalk widths apart lengthwise on the chalkboard.

Writing at the chalkboard

When writing calligraphy letters at the chalkboard, either hold the chalk lengthwise or hold two pieces at once. This will allow you to show the variation in width that takes place within each letter.

Letter formation

The Chancery cursive letters are like any type of alphabet in that they require practice to form the letters properly. If you are aware of the following common errors, you can help students learn to evaluate their own work.

1. *Pen angle*—Look for errors that result from an incorrect pen angle. For example, if serifs do not begin and end at 45°, then the pen angle is incorrect. And if the diagonal strokes are not thin, then the pen angle is incorrect.

2. *Slant*—Look for letters that do not have a 13° slant as indicated by the guide sheet slant lines. Uppercase and lowercase v, w, x, and z do not have any strokes that are on a 13° slant, but the letters should have the appearance of the 13° slant. If a student forces the letters to conform to the 13° slant, the letters will appear as shown below.

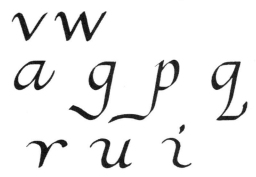

3. *Serifs*—Look for serifs on letters that should not have serifs or for serifs that are too long and too curved.

4. *Strokes*—Look for letters whose strokes were performed in the incorrect order or did not start and finish in the correct place.

5. *Shape*—Look for letters that are too thin, too wide, too square, too sharp, or too curved.

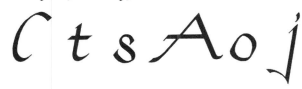

> It is important to recognize that the formation of calligraphy letters is as unique as any handwriting. Different calligraphers form letters according to the look of the letters and the preference of the designer.

Evaluation of Calligraphy

Although we do not recommend that the calligraphy lessons be graded, we do recommend that the students be taught to evaluate their own work as you guide them to look for the common errors mentioned in the section above.

Words to Work By

"The door to the room of success swings on the hinges of opposition."

"The test of your character is what it takes to stop you."

"You can do anything you ought to do."

"Blessed is the man who knows how to make stepping stones out of stumbling stones."

—taken from "Chapel Sayings of Dr. Bob Jones Sr."

Use with Lesson 1.

Pretest   name_____

Write the quotations.

Use with Lesson 1.   1

Materials and Preparation

Have available:

- Cursive handwriting charts.

Prepare:

- A cursive name model on the front of each student's worktext.
- A cursive name model for each student's desk.
- A copy of the letter to the parents for each student from the Appendix.
- The calligraphy guide sheets for each student.

Remove the insert from the center of each student worktext by tearing along the perforation, making two guide sheets. Tell the students to keep one copy of the guide sheet in their notebooks. Collect and store the spare sheet to have as an extra in case one is lost or gets worn out.

——— Lesson Content ———

Introduction

Introduce the student worktext and the theme—Tell the students that they will be improving their handwriting, as well as learning the Chancery style of lettering as they are introduced to various people and professions.

Instruct the students to turn to the table of contents. Introduce Penfellow, a sixth-century scribe, and Chanticleer, a notable member of the order *Galliformes*, the common, widely domesticated chicken. These characters will appear throughout the book. Read the limerick on the table of contents page and guide a discussion of the limerick and of the illustration of the two characters.

Next guide the students in an overview of the book. Tell them to read silently through the table of contents. As the students leaf through their books, point out the unit pages introducing the various professions and the Chancery

Digital Numerals   name_____

1 2 3 4 5 6 7 8 9 0

Answer the questions about the pictures, using the above numeral formations.

What is the telephone number showing on the phone?

555-1234

What is the time of the flight that was cancelled?

6:30

What is the total shown on the calculator?

198.00

What is the time shown on the computer screen?

9:42

2   Use with Lesson 1.

---

lessons at the end of each unit. Students may also look at the last unit, which concentrates on teaching uppercase letters, numerals, spacing, and layout in the Chancery style of lettering. Point out the sample writing selections as well as the calligraphy tips and glossary also included in the last unit.

Skill development

Guide a discussion of illustrations—Use the illustrations on the inside back cover of the student worktext to show correct posture, paper position, and pencil hold.

Demonstrate handwriting posture—Explain that the best handwriting posture is having the body bent slightly forward, not leaning to the left or to the right, with forearms resting on the desk. Check to see that each student is sitting comfortably in his chair with both feet on the floor. Be sure that each desk is slightly higher than the student's waist. Make notes about desk height problems so that seating assignments can be changed or mechanical adjustments made.

Demonstrate paper positioning—Paper should be positioned at a slant that approximately parallels the slant of the writing arm.

Demonstrate pencil hold—Pencils should be grasped lightly about an inch from the point.

Pretest

Guide the completion of the "Words to Work By" portion of the pretest on worktext pages iv and 1—Call attention to the illustration of Penfellow and Chanticleer leaving the castle. Discuss briefly the idea that the two characters are looking for a new profession.

Ask a student to read the quotations by Dr. Bob Jones Sr. Tell the class that he was a great evangelist and a very practical Christian. Help them to relate the content of the quotations to the theme of the book. Point out the name models attached to their desks. Instruct them to use the model as a guide as they neatly write their names on page 1.

Ask a student to read the instructions. Tell the students to refer to the cursive model on page iv as they complete page 1. Encourage them to do their best, but not to take too long. Stress that the page will not be graded or sent home but will be saved for them to see their progress as their handwriting improves during the year.

The cursive model of the quotations on worktext page iv will be used again in Lesson 66, which is the post-test.

Guide the completion of the "Digital Numerals" portion of the pretest on worktext page 2—Lead a brief discussion of the equipment illustrated and the digital displays that accompany them. Explain to the students that they will be writing cursive numerals rather than digital numerals. Tell them to refer to the cursive numeral models at the top of the page as they complete this part of the pretest.

Collect the papers. Make and record pertinent observations such as those listed below.

➤ Which letters or letter combinations are the most difficult for students to write and may require more than one lesson to review?

➤ Which students need additional activities at school and at home to strengthen fine-muscle coordination?

➤ Which students have trouble with alignment and spacing?

➤ Do any students have difficulty slanting consistently?

File the pretest so that you and your students can refer to it periodically in order to note progress.

You may want to send home the letter to the parents today. This will give an overall explanation of the handwriting program for the year.

Optional activity

Direct a writing activity—Read the following information to the students.

Most displays are visual although some, such as a fire alarm, can be auditory. Visual displays can be either digital or analogue. An analogue display shows the measurement increments such as on a clock face or thermometer. A digital display shows only the exact numbers involved using the digits 0-9.

Direct the students to list as many digital and analogue displays as they can. Point out the examples on page 2. *(Digital displays include the following: scoreboard, automobile odometer, display on photocopier, display on scales, clock, thermometer. Analogue displays include the following: clock, thermometer, and automobile speedometer.)*

People and Professions

Calligrapher and Astronomer

In *HANDWRITING 6 for Christian Schools*, cursive letters are largely presented in groups containing similar stroke patterns, and uppercase and lowercase letters are reviewed together. In this unit, two of the one o'clock letters, *c* and *a,* are presented in conjunction with the occupations of the calligrapher and the astronomer. Learning about the calligrapher will add depth to the student's introduction to calligraphy. Astronomy is an occupation of interest to all ages.

Please read the whole unit before beginning to teach it, noticing especially the last lesson on calligraphy. You may find it helpful at this time to begin practicing the strokes for the new calligraphy letters.

When I consider thy heavens, the work of thy fingers, the moon and the stars, which thou hast ordained; what is man, that thou art mindful of him?
—Psalm 8:3-4a

Materials and Preparation

Have available:

- A nib pen (optional).

Prepare:

- Handwriting lines on the chalkboard.

——— Lesson Content ———

Introduction

Introduce the unit—Tell the students to turn to worktext page 3. Point out that in this unit they will be learning about the work of the calligrapher and the astronomer. Mention that the word *calligraphy* comes from two Greek words that mean "beautiful writing." Tell the class that in the Far East calligraphy is done with a pointed brush instead of with the special pen that we use in our Western culture.

Show the nib pen. Explain that in past years, calligraphy was done with this type of pen or with a pen made from a broad-edged reed or with a quill. Today many people do fine work with a chisel-point pen. Ask a student to read the unit verse. Discuss how this verse relates to the work of an astronomer. *(He investigates the things that God has made in the heavens.)* If time permits, ask several students to describe how they feel when they look up and consider the star-filled sky. (BAT: 3a Self-concept)

Skill development

Review the formation of *c*—Point out that *calligrapher* begins with the letter *c*. Verbalize the direction of each stroke as you write the uppercase and lowercase letters on the chalkboard. Point out that the uppercase letter begins at one o'clock. Remind the students that both letters connect to the letters that follow them.

Begin at one,
Swing around to five.

Swing up and around to one,
Retrace and swing around to five.

Demonstrate the writing of *c*—Allow volunteers to write the following words on the chalkboard.

calligraphy	*parchment*	*decorative*
cursive	*curved*	

Demonstrate the writing of lowercase *c* in pairs—Point out that the pencil is not lifted between the letters. Tell the class to air-trace the letter *c* in pairs and then have several students practice writing pairs of the letter *c* on the chalkboard.

Demonstrate alternate styles of writing the letter *c* (optional).

The Calligrapher's Terminology

name_____

As early as the third century A.D., it was recorded that scribes noted for the speed and beauty of their handwriting often accompanied great men on their journeys. Contemporary scribes called calligraphers also engage in the art of fine handwriting. They are often employed by printers and publishers who recognize the beauty of their work.

Write the lettering term and its definition.

hook—a curved ending and beginning to strokes of an alphabet

pen nib—the removable tip of a lettering pen or fountain pen

swashes—long, decorative additions to letters

vellum—a fine grade of parchment paper prepared from lambskin, kidskin, or calfskin

4

Use with Lesson 2.

Guided practice

Direct attention to worktext page 4—Ask a student to read the title of the page and the paragraph about calligraphy. Explain to the students that on this page they will be writing information about lettering terms.

Focus on writing the letter *c*—Refer the students to the model letters at the top of worktext page 4. Point out the one o'clock starting position for the uppercase letter *c* and the cursive stroke at the beginning of the lowercase *c*.

Direct the completion of worktext page 4—Ask a student to read the directions. Encourage the students to use their best handwriting as they write each lettering term and its definition. Circulate among the students, checking posture, paper positioning, and pencil grip.

Optional activity

Direct an art activity—Read the following information.

> In 1843 Henry Cole commissioned John Calcott Horsley to design a Christmas scene to be printed on pasteboard. According to tradition, Cole commissioned the card because he was too busy with business that year to write to all his friends. One thousand of these cards were printed by Messrs. Jobbins of Warwick Court, Holborn. They printed the cards from a lithographic stone onto 5-by-3¼-inch pieces of pasteboard, which were then colored by hand. After the printers filled Henry Cole's order, the excess cards were sold by a printer, Joseph Cundall, at Summerly's Home Treasury Office, 12 Old Bond Street, London, for one shilling each. Mr. Cole's printed Christmas greeting was the first Christmas card.

Point out that we can see examples of beautiful handwriting printed on cards. Direct each student to design and prepare a greeting card—Christmas or birthday. Remind him to use his best handwriting.

The Astronomer's Telescopes

name_____

Using powerful telescopes, astronomers study the sun, moons, and planets in our solar system. They are also able to observe distant galaxies and stars. With what they observe, they are able to predict events such as eclipses, comet sightings, and even the interference of sunspots on our communication systems.

Write the information about two of the world's largest telescopes.

The Hubble telescope orbits the earth and allows views of space that are unavailable from telescopes on the earth's surface.

This is an aerial view of the world's largest fixed-dish radio telescope, located near Arecibo, Puerto Rico.

Arecibo Radio Observatory National Astronomy & Ionosphere Center

Use with Lesson 3.   5

Materials and Preparation

Prepare:

- Handwriting lines on the chalkboard.

——— Lesson Content ———

Introduction

Relate the following information.

One of the astronomer's most important tools is the telescope. An early refractor telescope was used by Galileo in 1609 to look at the surface of the moon. He mounted two lenses at each end of a tube and adjusted them to focus the image. More than a hundred years later, Sir Isaac Newton developed the reflector telescope, which uses mirrors to reflect the light. Astronomers today can look into a composite telescope, which is a combination of both mirrors and lenses. Modern electronics has helped scientists develop radio telescopes. These can reach much farther into space than ordinary telescopes, and they help astronomers obtain information about our galaxy.

Skill development

Review the formation of *a*—Verbalize the direction of each stroke as you write the letters on the chalkboard. Remind the students that the letter *a* connects to letters that follow.

***Begin at one,
Swing around to lock,
Retrace and curve.***

***Swing up and around to one,
Retrace and swing around to lock,
Retrace and curve.***

Demonstrate the writing of *a*—Allow several students to write the following words on the chalkboard.

astronomy   *planet*   *Arizona*
stars   *refractor*

Demonstrate the writing of lowercase *a* in pairs—Point out that the pencil is not lifted between letters. Tell the class to air-trace the letter *a* in pairs, and then allow several students to practice writing pairs of the letter *a* on the chalkboard.

Demonstrate alternate styles of writing the letter *a* (optional).

Guided practice

Direct attention to worktext page 5—Ask a student to read the introductory paragraph about telescopes.

Focus on writing the letter *a*—Refer the students to the model letters at the top of worktext page 5. Point out the one o'clock starting position for both uppercase and lowercase *a*.

Direct the completion of worktext page 5—Ask another student to read the directions. Instruct the students to write the information about the two telescopes on the lines provided.

Optional activity

Direct a writing activity—Instruct each student to write one or two stanzas of the poem "The Star" by Jane Taylor (*Favorite Poems Old and New,* edited by Helen Ferris).

An Astronomical Task

name_____

Write the letters and words, using correct alignment.

Handwriting Tips

Alignment is the correct placement of letters in relation to the base line.

C C

c c

calligrapher

a a

a a

astronomer

Alphabetize each column of words on the lines below.

celestial   angle   reflector
comet   alignment   refractor
cluster   ascender   meteor
cosmology   alphabet   galaxy
chromatic   accuracy   planet

celestial	accuracy	galaxy
chromatic	alignment	meteor
cluster	alphabet	planet
comet	angle	reflector
cosmology	ascender	refractor

6   **Use with Lesson 4.**

Materials and Preparation

Prepare:

- Handwriting lines on the chalkboard.
- The following words on the chalkboard.

      calligrapher   *astronomer*

——— Lesson Content ———

Introduction

Create interest in the lesson—Instruct a volunteer to read the title of the lesson. Ask the students what kind of job would be *astronomical*. Elicit the idea that it would be a really big job. Tell them that an astronomical unit of length is equal to the distance between the sun and the earth, about 93 million miles, and that the term *astronomical* is used to describe something that is really big. Bring out the idea that the word *astronomical* is derived from the Greek word for star—*astro*.

Skill development

Focus on the handwriting tip on worktext page 6—Ask a student to read aloud the handwriting tip in the box at the top of the page. Call attention to the incorrect alignment samples. Remind the students that the letters should rest on the base line. Point out the words on the chalkboard and emphasize the proper alignment of the letters.

Guided practice

Focus on writing the letters *c* and *a*—Direct a student to read the directions at the top of worktext page 6. Remind the students that uppercase *c* and *a* begin at one o'clock. Also point out that all four letters connect to the letters that follow them. Instruct the students to trace the gray letter models and then to practice the letters and words on the lines provided.

Direct the completion of worktext page 6—Ask each of three students to read a list. Direct the students to tell the correct alphabetical order for the first list. Instruct them to number the words in alphabetical order before writing them on the lines. Continue with the other lists.

Optional activity

Direct a research activity—Give the students the following information about an astronomical instrument.

> A coelostat is an arrangement of mirrors driven by clockwork so as to reflect sunlight vertically down a hollow tube to a telescope. This arrangement of mirrors prevents the telescope from having to be pointed directly at the sun.

Direct each student to look up the word *coelenterate* in a dictionary and write its definition. Then tell him to write a sentence that explains what the definition of *coelenterate* has in common with the definition of *coelostat*. (The word *coelenterate* means "hollow intestines." Both of the words have the prefix *coel-*, meaning "hollow.")

The Lights in the Heavens

name_____

"And God made two great lights; the greater light to rule the day, and the lesser light to rule the night: he made the stars also."

—*Genesis 1:16*

"He telleth the number of the stars; he calleth them all by their names."

Psalm 147:4

"Which maketh Arcturus, Orion, and Pleiades, and the chambers of the south. Which doeth great things past finding out: yea, and wonders without number."

Job 9:9–10

Self-evaluation	s	n
Posture		
Paper Positioning		
Pencil Hold		
Letter Formation		
Alignment		
Slant		
Spacing		
Neatness		

s=satisfactory   n=needs improvement

Write the verses on the lines below.

Use with Lesson 5.   7

© 2000 BJU Press. Reproduction prohibited.

Corel Corporation

Materials and Preparation

Have available:

- An evaluation form for each student.

Prepare:

- Handwriting lines on the chalkboard.

——— Lesson Content ———

Introduction

Relate the following information.

The Bible tells us that there are too many stars to count. As astronomers develop better equipment, they are finding more and more stars. In 1603, John Bayer introduced a systematic way of identifying particular stars within a constellation. He assigned the first letter of the Greek alphabet, *alpha,*

to the brightest star of the constellation. He used the second letter, *beta,* to name the second brightest star, and so on until he had used up all the letters in the Greek alphabet. Then he continued with the letters of the Roman alphabet. He also made star charts that included maps of the constellations.

Skill development

Review the formation of *c* and *a*—Verbalize the direction of the strokes as you write each uppercase and lowercase letter on the chalkboard.

See pages ix-xii for the stroke descriptions.

Ask how the uppercase letters are similar. *(They begin at the one o'clock position.)* Ask how all four letters are alike. *(They all connect to the letters that follow them.)* Ask volunteers to write the following sentences on the chalkboard.

Contemporary scribes are called calligraphers.

Astronomers cannot call all the stars by name.

Assessment

Direct attention to worktext page 7—Tell the class that these Bible verses refer to some of the constellations that John Bayer charted.

Direct attention to the self-evaluation chart on worktext page 7—Explain to the students that after writing the Scripture verses on this page they will evaluate their own handwriting. Explain that they will check the *s* column if they feel they have performed the handwriting skill satisfactorily. If the skill was neglected, they will check the *n* column.

Guide the completion of worktext page 7—Ask several students to read the directions and the verses. Tell the students to write the verses. Encourage them to do their best because you will also evaluate this page. (BAT: 2e Diligence)

You may want to use the evaluation form in the Appendix with this lesson. Be aware that the back of this page will be used in the next lesson on calligraphy.

Optional activity

Direct a writing activity—Read the following information to the students.

Of all the scriptural references to stars, perhaps the most intriguing are the references to the "star of wonder." What exactly was the "star of wonder" that the wise men saw in the east? In order to speculate as to the nature of that special star, we need to establish two things: the time of Christ's birth and the appearance of the skies at the time of Christ's birth.

First, let's establish the time of the birth of Christ. The Scripture tells us that Christ was born in the days of Herod the king, and history establishes the death of Herod in 4 B.C.; therefore, Christ's birth was sometime before 4 B.C. But how long before 4 B.C.? Another clue from Scripture will help us determine this. The Scripture says that Christ was born at a time of taxation by Caesar Augustus. According to a list of the years that decrees for tax collection were issued, 8 B.C. is the only year near the time under discussion. So Christ was born sometime after 8 B.C. but before 4 B.C. Also, it was probably in the spring since that is the time when lambs are born and shepherds "keep watch over their flock by night."

The second thing to consider is the appearance of the skies at the time of Christ's birth. Did the wise men see a star, a meteor, a comet, or a planet? The Greek word for *star* can mean any one of those things. It could not have been a meteor because meteors burn up in a flash of light in just a few seconds and that does not agree with the description we have in Scripture. Nor could it have been a comet because at that time comets were viewed as evil omens of war, pestilence, or famine—not good signs. Furthermore, although an unusual grouping of the planets Jupiter, Saturn, and Mars did happen in the year 6 B.C., a description of this grouping does not fit with the scriptural account either. Therefore, we are left with the possibility that the wise men saw a special star. And special it was, for Scripture says that before they came to Herod, they saw "his star in the east" and that after they left Herod, they "saw the star" which caused them to rejoice "with exceeding great joy." Apparently they had not seen the star after they left the east and were astonished to see it again. The Scripture also says that "the star, which they saw in the east, went before them." Literally that means that the star was going before them until it came and stood over where the little child was. A natural star could not have done what that verse describes. It was also special because apparently only the wise men saw it; else why would Herod have "enquired of them diligently what time the star appeared," and how could the wise men follow it to the place of Christ's birth when Herod couldn't?

Direct the students to write the following verses about the star: Matthew 2:2, 7, 9, and 10.

Calligraphy Letters c and a

name_____

Calligraphy Tips

Concentrate on using the proper pen hold, paper position, and body position.

c a

Copy the practice strokes.

////

≡

(((

))))

≋

≋

Write the letters *c* and *a*.

c c c

a a a

8   Use with Lesson 6.

© 2000 BJU Press. Reproduction prohibited.

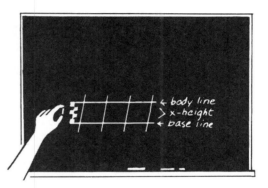

Because of ease of use, we highly recommend using an overhead projector for the calligraphy lessons. However, there are additional options. You may use the overhead pen with a white board. You will need to draw two lines five pen tip widths apart as a guide. Add a few slant lines at 13°. You may also use the chalkboard. For this you will need to draw two lines five chalk widths apart and add a few slant lines at 13°. The chalk is held lengthwise for lettering.

← body line
← x-height
← base line

——— Lesson Content ———

Introduction

Explain the calligraphy sections in the worktext—Show the students the two sections of their worktexts where they can find calligraphy information.

First, point out that there is a lowercase calligraphy lesson at the end of each unit. Direct the students to look briefly at pages 14 and 20 as examples.

Then direct them to the calligraphy unit which starts on page 81. Allow them to leaf through the pages and notice the following things:

➤ The calligraphy lowercase review on pages 82-83.
➤ The calligraphy uppercase lessons on pages 84-96.
➤ The calligraphy numeral lesson on page 97.
➤ The spacing and layout lessons on pages 98-99.
➤ The calligraphy examples on pages 100-103.
➤ The calligraphy reference pages (Calligraphy Glossary and Calligraphy Tips) on pages 104-6.

Direct a closer look at page 104—Direct the students to the Calligraphy Glossary on page 104 of their worktext. Discuss with them the definitions of *calligraphy* and *Chancery cursive.*

Materials and Preparation

Have available:

• A chisel-point pen for each student.

Before distributing the pens, tape students' names or initials to the pens in order to assure their return to the correct student. To avoid loss or overuse of the pens, you may want to collect the pens after each lesson.

• A guide sheet for each student.
• A piece of typing paper for each student.
• Worktext page 8 for each student if previously collected for assessment of page 7.
• An overhead projector.
• An overhead pen (the kind with a wide, flat edge) to use on the overhead projector.

Prepare:

• A transparency of the lowercase guide sheet.

You may wish to point out that the word *cursive* is from the Latin meaning "flowing." It usually refers to "writing with a running hand so that the characters are rapidly formed without raising the pen and in consequence have their angles rounded and separate strokes joined and at length become slanted" (*Oxford English Dictionary*). In ancient manuscripts, however, the "cursive style" could refer to printing that showed some of these characteristics.

Then direct the students to read the definition of *guide sheet*. Tell them to close their books while you demonstrate the definition.

Illustrate the parts of the guide sheet as mentioned in its definition—Hold up a guide sheet so that the side labeled "Lowercase Guide Sheet" faces the students. Trace a base line and a body line with your finger. Explain that these lines are two of the five guidelines that indicate the height of each stroke. Tell them that they will learn about the other three guidelines when they do the Chancery cursive uppercase letters and numerals.

Now indicate the x-height. Tell the students that *x-height* refers to the distance between the base and body lines and that it is always equal to five pen tip widths. Explain that even without a guide sheet or with a different-sized pen, they can figure out the proper x-height by marking a distance of five pen tip widths on a piece of typing paper.

Again, hold up the guide sheet with the side labeled "Lowercase Guide Sheet" facing the students. Trace a slant line with your finger. Explain that these lines are there to indicate the proper slant (13°) of each stroke. This is not to be confused with the 45° pen angle which is the angle of the chisel point (flat edge) of the pen to the horizontal edge of the paper. (See proper position under Skill Development.)

Explain that they will use the lowercase guide sheet as they learn their lowercase Chancery cursive letters. Show them the advanced guide sheet and explain to them that they will use it when they learn the Chancery cursive uppercase letters and numerals. You may desire to point out that all five guidelines are on the advanced guide sheet.

Finally, review the new terms. Review the parts of a guide sheet *(the slant lines, the x-height, and these two guidelines: the base and body lines)* and the use of a guide sheet *(to control the height and slant of each stroke)*.

Illustrate the use of a guide sheet as mentioned in its definition—Place a guide sheet under a piece of typing paper and hold the paper and guide sheet up to show the students how the lines from the guide sheet can be seen through the paper to help direct the height and slant of their strokes.

Skill development

Demonstrate the proper positions mentioned on work-text pages 105-6—Distribute the chisel pen and a piece of typing paper to each student. Instruct him to lay these aside for later use. Direct the students to the Calligraphy Tips on pages 105-6. Read and demonstrate the tips about proper body position, paper position, and pen hold. Tell the students to imitate you as you demonstrate. Stress the importance of locking the cap on the pen whenever it is not in use to keep the pen from drying out.

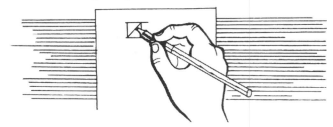

Read and demonstrate the tip about the proper pen angle. Review the fact just established that the proper pen position is upright, but now add the fact that the chisel point of the pen should be positioned at a 45° angle to the horizontal edge of the paper. Demonstrate how to draw a small box on the top of their paper with a diagonal line from the top right corner to the bottom left corner. Then show them how to place their pen on this line to determine a 45° angle. Stress the point that this one rule will make a big difference between well-formed letters and letters that have little resemblance to the correct form.

Review three confusing concepts—Explain that with a pen positioned upright and the chisel point positioned at a 45° angle, they will write strokes slanted 13°. Direct the students to set aside their pens, paper, and guide sheets as you demonstrate the strokes and letters.

Demonstrate the practice strokes—Using the guidelines on the overhead, demonstrate the practice strokes shown on student worktext page 8.

You may either write directly on the transparency of the guide sheet or place the transparency under another piece of acetate to use as a guide.

Explain to the students that these strokes are the basic strokes for all of the Chancery cursive letters. Tell them that practicing these strokes will help them to form better letters.

Demonstrate the formation of lowercase *c* and *a*—Verbalize the direction of each stroke as you write the letters on the lines on the overhead. Tell the students to be sure to use the whole edge of the chisel point or their strokes will be thin and straggly. Point out that both letters begin at the one o'clock position and that the letters should not connect to the letters that follow. Remind them that the definition of *cursive* can refer to letters that are not connected but have other characteristics of the cursive style. They will have a natural tendency to connect some letters. Connecting letters is acceptable in some cases, but try to limit it until the students are writing the strokes for the letters in the correct order and starting at the correct o'clock position.

**Curve up,
Swing around.**

**Glide left,
Swing around to lock,
Retrace and curve.**

Guided practice

Direct handwriting on worktext page 8—Review the calligraphy tip at the top of the page. Direct attention to the practice strokes. Then refer the students to the letter models on the lines at the bottom of the page. Read the following procedures for practicing the letters at the bottom of the page.

1. Note the arrow that indicates the direction of each stroke.
2. Trace the black letter with your finger.
3. Trace the gray letters with your pen.

Walk around the classroom to check that the students are making the correct strokes, both for practice strokes and for letter formation. Point out that the 45° angle of their pens will cause their letters to go above and below the line a bit. Encourage them to place their letters as much in the center of the guidelines as possible.

Refer to the Calligraphy Introduction on pages xxi-xxix.

Continued practice

Tell the students to continue to practice with typing paper and a guide sheet—Direct the students to place their lowercase guide sheet under a piece of typing paper and continue to practice their strokes and letters.

People and Professions

Oceanographer and Quarrier

Two more one o'clock letters, *o* and *q,* are reviewed in this unit. The occupations oceanographer and quarrier both have an aura of mystery that will be intriguing to the student.

You will want to preview the entire unit now, concentrating especially on the calligraphy lesson. Practice is essential to your learning the strokes for the new calligraphy letters.

Materials and Preparation

Have available:

- Handwriting paper for each student.

Prepare:

- Handwriting lines on the chalkboard.

——— Lesson Content ———

Introduction

Introduce the unit—Tell the class to turn to worktext page 9. Use questions such as the following to discuss the page.

1. What occupations will be studied in this unit?
2. What do you think an oceanographer does? *(studies the ocean)*
3. What do you think a quarrier does? *(digs stone from a quarry)*
4. Read the unit verse to yourself. What occupation do you think it refers to? *(oceanographer)* Why? *(These words suggest the ocean: sea, ships, wonders in the deep.)*

After the discussion, point out that both the oceanographer and the quarrier work closely with something that the Lord has created and therefore have an excellent opportunity to observe His wonders.

Direct attention to worktext page 10—Ask a student to read the information about an oceanographer at the top of the page.

Skill development

Review the formation of *o*—Verbalize the direction of each stroke as you write the letters on the chalkboard. Remind the students that lowercase *o* connects to letters that follow but that uppercase *o* does not.

***Begin at one,
Swing around to lock
and curl.***

15

Swing up and around to one,
Retrace and swing around to lock,
Sweep out.

Demonstrate the writing of *o*—Tell the class to air-trace the lowercase *o,* and then allow volunteers to write the following words on the chalkboard.

ocean	*forward*
shore	*Atlantic Ocean*
move	

Demonstrate the writing of lowercase *o* in pairs—Point out that the pencil is not lifted between the letters. Direct the class to air-trace the letter *o* in pairs, and then allow several students to practice writing pairs of the letter *o* on the chalkboard.

Demonstrate alternate styles of writing the letter *o* (optional).

Guided practice

Focus on writing the letter *o*—Refer the students to the model letters at the top of worktext page 10. Point out the one o'clock starting position for uppercase *o* and the cursive stroke at the beginning of the lowercase *o*.

Direct the completion of worktext page 10—Have volunteers read the directions and the two paragraphs. Instruct the students to write the paragraphs about the ocean on handwriting paper.

Optional activity

Guide a discussion about scientists—Point out to the students that many other scientists besides oceanographers are also interested in the oceans.

Write the following list of types of scientists on the chalkboard.

physicist	*chemist*
marine biologist	*meteorologist*

Read each of the following statements and tell the students to choose from the list on the chalkboard which type of scientist each statement refers to. The items from the list can be used more than once.

1. He investigates the forms of plant and animal life in the oceans. *(marine biologist)*
2. He studies the influence of the oceans on weather and climate. *(meteorologist)*
3. He studies new methods of recovering minerals from water. *(chemist)*
4. He attempts to produce electricity from the energy of the tides. *(physicist)*
5. He attempts to find an economical way to produce drinking water from sea water. *(chemist)*

Point out that many other people besides scientists are interested in the oceans. Refer to the verses written on worktext page 9. Then list on the chalkboard the following areas of ocean-related businesses.

weather	*minerals*
transportation	*recreation*
food	

Ask for examples of ways that these areas are connected with the ocean. For example, a cruise ship, an ocean-going vessel, was designed for recreation and transportation.

Quarrying for Granite

A quarrier digs, cuts, and blasts stone in an open pit, or quarry.

Vermont Travel Division

Write the outline on handwriting paper.

I. Crushed stone
    A. Procedure for crushing stone
       1. Explosives set off in holes
       2. Stone crushed in crusher plant
    B. Purposes for crushed stone
       1. Used in concrete
       2. Used in road building
II. Dimension stone
    A. Procedure for cutting stone
       1. Large blocks cut by machine
       2. Small blocks cut with wedges
    B. Purposes for cut stone
       1. Used in buildings
       2. Used in monuments

Use with Lesson 8.   11

Materials and Preparation

Prepare:

- Fourteen handwriting lines on the chalkboard for the outlining activity.
- The following words on the chalkboard.

      quarrier   *Canfield Quarry*

——— Lesson Content ———

Introduction

Relate the following information about quarrying.

The quarrier uses several different kinds of equipment to help him with his job. One important item is a feather, a piece of steel that is rounded on one side and flat on the other. Feathers are used with wedges and a drill in an operation called "plug and feather" which breaks up the rock into chunks. The quarrier also uses the drill to make holes for explosives if he wants to shatter the rock. The channeling machine is a much larger piece of quarry equipment. It looks like a small locomotive, but it has long chisels on its sides. As the channeling machine moves along a track, it chisels slowly into the rock, sometimes cutting as deeply as ten feet.

Point out that on the worktext page the students will learn about two kinds of stone that the quarrier can produce with this equipment.

Direct attention to worktext page 11—Ask a student to read the sentence about the quarrier at the top of the page.

Skill development

Review outline form—Remind the students that major points in an outline have a Roman numeral or an uppercase letter before them and that these points in an outline can be complete sentences or phrases. Tell them that smaller points in an outline have an Arabic numeral before them. Write the Roman numerals, uppercase letters, and Arabic numerals in the correct form on the chalkboard.

Example:

I.
    A.
       1.
       2.
    B.
       1.
       2.
II.
    A.
       1.
       2.
    B.
       1.
       2.

Review the formation of *q*—Verbalize the direction of each stroke as you write the letters on the chalkboard.

**(1) Begin at one,
Swing around to lock.
(2) Curve and slash.**

**Swing up and around to one,
Retrace and swing around to lock,
Drop low,
Curve right and up to lock,
Bounce.**

Point out that the uppercase letter begins at one o'clock. Direct attention to the words on the chalkboard. Tell the students to note that uppercase *q* connects to letters that follow.

Demonstrate the writing of *q*—Tell the class to air-trace the letters. Allow several students to write the words on the chalkboard, using your examples as models.

Demonstrate alternate styles of writing the letter *q* (optional).

Guided practice

Focus on writing the letter *q*—Refer the students to the model letters at the top of worktext page 11. Remind them that both uppercase and lowercase *q* connect to letters that follow.

Guide the completion of the outline activity on worktext page 11—Instruct a student to read the outline about quarrying. Ask another student to read the directions. As the students complete the page, walk around the classroom to check correct outline form.

Optional activity

Direct a writing activity—Explain to the students that both rocks and minerals are quarried. Tell them that minerals are pure substances (either elements or compounds) whereas rocks are mixtures of minerals. Explain that this activity is about minerals only. Copy the following Scripture references for the students.

> Ezra 8:27 *(copper and gold)*
> Psalm 19:10 *(gold)*
> Daniel 2:33 *(iron)*
> Jeremiah 6:29 *(lead)*
> Genesis 23:16 *(silver)*
> Isaiah 1:25 *(tin)*
> Revelation 21:18 *(jasper and gold)*
> Genesis 2:12 *(onyx)*
> Exodus 24:10 *(sapphire)*

Direct each student to look up each reference and to write the name of the mineral mentioned next to its reference. Encourage him to look up each mineral in a dictionary and to write a sentence about the use of that mineral next to its name.

Materials and Preparation

Have available:

- A globe or a map of the world.

Prepare:

- Handwriting lines on the chalkboard.
- The following words on the chalkboard.

  oceanographer   *quarrier*

——— Lesson Content ———

Introduction

Direct attention to the map displayed—Help the students find on the globe or map as many oceans and seas as time permits. Examples are the Antarctic Ocean, Arctic Ocean, Atlantic Ocean, Indian Ocean, Pacific Ocean, Aegean Sea, Baltic Sea, Bering Sea, Black Sea, Caribbean Sea, China Sea, Irish Sea, Sea of Japan, Mediterranean Sea, and Red Sea. Mention that oceanographers do their work in oceans all over the world.

Skill development

Focus on the handwriting tip at the top of worktext page 12—Ask a student to read aloud the handwriting tip in the box at the top of the page. Remind the students that uppercase and tall letters should not run into descenders from the line above. Point out the words on the chalkboard. Then write *Atlantic Ocean* below *oceanographer,* demonstrating that the tall letters do not run into the descenders. Next write *Camton Quarry* directly below *quarrier,* running the *c* of *Camton* into the *q* of *quarrier.* Point out the importance of remembering this handwriting tip.

Guided practice

Focus on writing the letters *o* and *q*—Direct a student to read the directions at the top of worktext page 12. Remind the students that uppercase *o* and *q* begin at one o'clock and that uppercase *q* and lowercase *o* and *q* connect to the letters that follow them. Instruct the students to practice the letters and words on the lines provided and to watch for descenders.

Direct the completion of the crossword puzzle on worktext page 12—Ask a student to read the directions. Remind the students that sometimes it is better to use a printing style. Instruct the students to use PreCursive letters to complete the puzzle.

Optional activity

Direct a writing activity—Instruct each student to use the terms from the puzzle on worktext page 12 to write sentences. Encourage him to use as many of the terms in one sentence as he can.

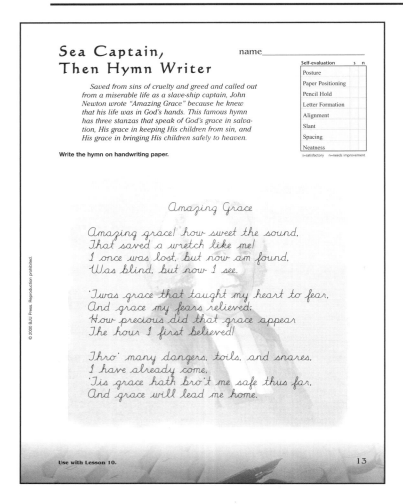

Sea Captain,
Then Hymn Writer

name_____

Saved from sins of cruelty and greed and called out
from a miserable life as a slave-ship captain, John
Newton wrote "Amazing Grace" because he knew
that his life was in God's hands. This famous hymn
has three stanzas that speak of God's grace in salvation, His grace in keeping His children from sin, and
His grace in bringing His children safely to heaven.

Self-evaluation	s	n
Posture		
Paper Positioning		
Pencil Hold		
Letter Formation		
Alignment		
Slant		
Spacing		
Neatness		

s=satisfactory   n=needs improvement

Write the hymn on handwriting paper.

Amazing Grace

Amazing grace! how sweet the sound,
That saved a wretch like me!
I once was lost, but now am found,
Was blind, but now I see.

'Twas grace that taught my heart to fear,
And grace my fears relieved;
How precious did that grace appear
The hour I first believed!

Thro' many dangers, toils, and snares,
I have already come;
'Tis grace hath bro't me safe thus far,
And grace will lead me home.

Use with Lesson 10.   13

© 2000 BJU Press. Reproduction prohibited.

Materials and Preparation

Have available:

- Handwriting paper for each student.

Prepare:

- Handwriting lines on the chalkboard.

———— Lesson Content ————

Introduction

Relate the following information about John Newton.

John Newton lived from 1725-1807. Although he was rebellious and proud in his early years, God had a plan for his life. John was kidnapped and forced to become a sailor when he was only fourteen years old. He was whipped when he tried to desert the ship and ended up as a white slave on an island off the coast of Africa. At last he was rescued by a sea captain sent by his father; but trouble struck again, and he almost drowned in a terrible storm on the way back to England. God used these

and other hardships to make John start thinking about spiritual things. He finally surrendered his life to the Lord when he was thirty years old, and later he became a preacher.

Direct attention to worktext page 13—Ask a student to read the information about John Newton at the top of the page.

Skill development

Review the formation of *o* and *q*—Verbalize the direction of the strokes as you write each uppercase and lowercase letter on the chalkboard.

See pages ix-xii for the stroke descriptions.

Ask how the uppercase letters are similar. *(They begin at one o'clock.)* Ask how the lowercase letters are alike. *(They begin with a cursive stroke up and around to one.)*

Assessment

Direct attention to the self-evaluation chart on worktext page 13—Remind the students that after writing the hymn on this page they will evaluate their own handwriting on the chart.

Guide the completion of worktext page 13—Allow volunteers to read the directions and the three stanzas of "Amazing Grace." Encourage the students to do their best as they write the hymn on handwriting paper. Then lead the class in singing the hymn together.

You may want to use the evaluation form in the Appendix with this lesson. Be aware that the back of this page will be used in the next lesson on calligraphy.

Optional activity

Direct a writing activity—Read the following information about the Reverend Hopper, the author of the hymn "Jesus, Saviour, Pilot Me."

Like John Newton, the Reverend Hopper was a man who knew the life of the sea and later wrote hymns. The Reverend Hopper was from a seafaring family and also ministered to many seamen at the Church of Sea and Land in the New York Harbor. His hymns directly reflect his knowledge of the sea; therefore, they had a great appeal to seafaring men.

Provide a copy of the words to the hymn "Jesus, Saviour, Pilot Me" for each student.

> Jesus, Saviour, pilot me,
> Over life's tempestuous sea;
> Unknown waves before me roll,
> Hiding rock and treacherous shoal;
> Chart and compass come from Thee,
> Jesus, Saviour, pilot me.

Direct each student to read the hymn carefully and use a dictionary and a Bible to answer the following questions on handwriting paper.

1. What is the meaning of the word *tempestuous?* *(stormy)*
2. What is the meaning of the word *shoal? (shallow water)*
3. At the end of verse 1 the Reverend Hopper wrote, "Chart and compass come from Thee." What does that mean? *(Jesus will guide us.)*
4. What passage of Scripture tells the story in which Jesus says "Peace, be still" to the waves? *(Mark 4:39)*
5. What is the meaning of the word *sovereign? (having supreme rank or power)*

Lesson 11   Calligraphy Letters *o* and *e*   Worktext, page 14

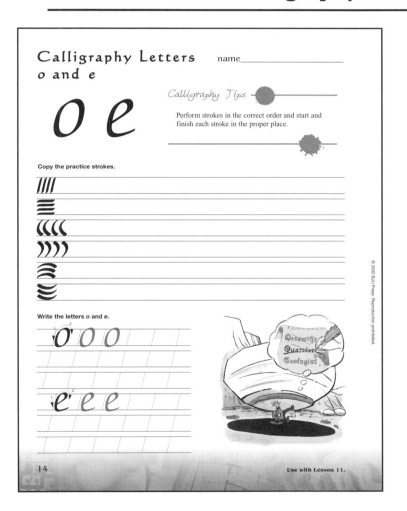

Materials and Preparation

Have available:

- A chisel-point pen for each student.
- A guide sheet for each student.
- A piece of typing paper for each student.
- A transparency of the lowercase guide sheet.
- An overhead projector.
- An overhead pen.

—— Lesson Content ——

Introduction

Review some of the terms listed on worktext page 104—Direct the students to turn to the Calligraphy Glossary on page 104 in their worktexts. Review the meaning of the terms related to the guide sheet. *(the slant lines, the x-height, and these two guidelines: base and body lines)* Then review the reason for using the guide sheet. *(to control the height and slant of each stroke)*

Skill development

Review some of the tips listed on worktext pages 105-6—After handing out a pen and piece of typing paper to each student, direct their attention to Calligraphy Tips on pages 105-6 in the worktext. Read and demonstrate the tips about proper body position, paper position, and pen hold. Have the students imitate you as you demonstrate. Stress the importance of locking the cap on the pen whenever it is not in use to keep the pen from drying out.

Read and demonstrate the tip about proper pen angle. Remind the students to draw a small box with a diagonal line from the top right corner to the bottom left corner to help them determine the 45° angle of the chisel point to the horizontal edge of the paper. Direct them to set aside their pens, paper, and guide sheets as you demonstrate the strokes and letters.

Read the tip about proper breath control—Explain to the students that if they either hold their breath or breathe out when they write, they will have smoother-looking letters.

Review the practice strokes—Using the overhead pen, write the practice strokes on the lines on the overhead or white board.

21

Demonstrate the formation of lowercase *o* and *e*—Write the letters on the lines on the transparency, verbalizing the direction of each stroke as you write. Point out that both letters begin at the eleven o'clock position. Remind the students that the letters should not connect to the letters that follow.

(1) Swing around left.
(2) Swing around right.

(1) Swing around left.
(2) Swing around right to halfway between base line and body line.

Guided practice

Direct handwriting on worktext page 14—Direct the students to set aside their guide sheet and typing paper for additional practice later. Review the calligraphy tip at the top of the page. Direct attention to the practice strokes. Refer the students to the letter models on the lines at the bottom of the page. Remind them of the following procedures for practicing the letters at the bottom of the page.

1. Note the arrow that indicates the direction of each stroke.
2. Trace the black letter with your finger.
3. Trace the gray letters with your pen.

Walk around the classroom to check that the students are making the correct strokes, both for practice strokes and for letter formation. Look for common errors.

Refer to the Calligraphy Introduction on pages xxi-xxix.

Continued practice

Direct practice with typing paper and a guide sheet—Remind the students to use the side of the guide sheet labeled "Lowercase Guide Sheet." Tell each student to write the practice strokes, new letters, and the letters that were taught in the last calligraphy lesson (*c* and *a*). Be sure to collect the pens when the students have finished.

PEOPLE AND PROFESSIONS

Geologist and Engineer

The letters *g* and *e* will be reviewed in this unit, and the occupations of the geologist and the engineer have been chosen to represent them. Students interested in earth science or construction will be challenged by the introductory and optional activities in these lessons.

Be sure to read the entire unit to prepare yourself for teaching, especially noting the calligraphy lesson. Time spent now in practicing the calligraphy skills will add greatly to your proficiency when teaching the lesson.

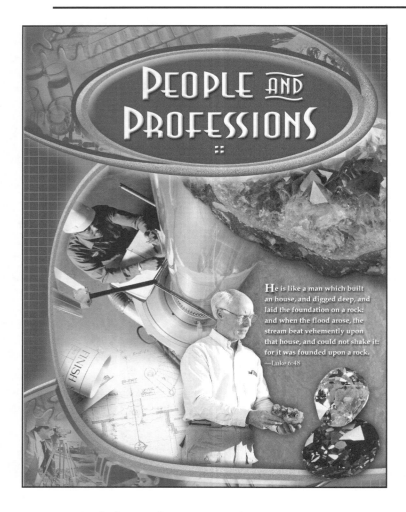

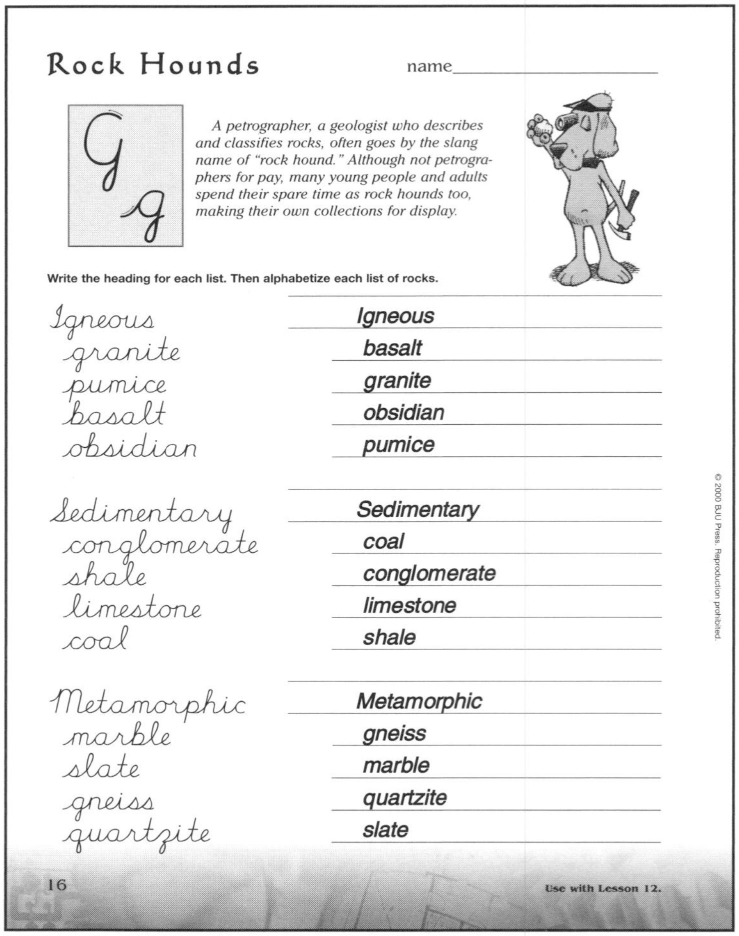

Rock Hounds

name_____

A petrographer, a geologist who describes and classifies rocks, often goes by the slang name of "rock hound." Although not petrographers for pay, many young people and adults spend their spare time as rock hounds too, making their own collections for display.

Write the heading for each list. Then alphabetize each list of rocks.

(handwritten)	(printed)
Igneous	Igneous
granite	basalt
pumice	granite
basalt	obsidian
obsidian	pumice
Sedimentary	Sedimentary
conglomerate	coal
shale	conglomerate
limestone	limestone
coal	shale
Metamorphic	Metamorphic
marble	gneiss
slate	marble
gneiss	quartzite
quartzite	slate

16   Use with Lesson 12.

Materials and Preparation

Prepare:

- Handwriting lines on the chalkboard.
- The following words on the chalkboard.

  geologist   engineer

—— Lesson Content ——

Introduction

Introduce the unit—Direct attention to the words on the chalkboard. Elicit the meaning of the word *geologist* from its derivation, *geo* (earth) and *logos* (study). After discussing what an engineer does, ask the students to give examples of the kinds of things that engineers help to build. Tell the class to turn to worktext page 15, and ask a volunteer to read the verse aloud.

Relate the following information.

The rock in this verse pictures Christ as the safe, solid foundation for a person's life. You can find other Bible references to Christ as the Rock. In Ephesians 2:20, Paul describes the Lord Jesus as the chief Cornerstone, the most important part of the church's foundation. (BAT: 3e Unity of Christ and the church) For unbelievers, Matthew 21:44 refers to Christ as the crushing stone of judgment. (BAT: 7a Grace)

Direct attention to worktext page 16—Ask a student to read the information at the top of the page. Remind the students of the three basic types of rock: igneous (formed from cooled lava), sedimentary (formed in layers under water), metamorphic (formed when other rocks are changed by heat or pressure).

Skill development

Review the formation of *g*—Verbalize the direction of each stroke as you write the letters on the chalkboard. Point out that uppercase *g* begins at the one o'clock position. Tell the students to note that uppercase and lowercase *g* connect to the letters that follow them.

Begin at one,
Swing around to three,
Drop low and loop.

Swing up and around to one,
Retrace and swing around to lock,
Drop low and loop.

Demonstrate the writing of lowercase *g* in pairs—Point out that the pencil is not lifted between letters. Tell the class to air-trace the letters, and then allow students to write the following words on the chalkboard.

giggle   bragging   beggar   luggage

Demonstrate alternate styles of writing the letter *g* (optional).

Guided practice

Guide the completion of worktext page 16—Ask volunteers to read the names of the rocks listed. If time permits, give the following information about the less familiar rocks.

pumice—a porous, lightweight volcanic rock

basalt—a hard, dense, dark volcanic rock

obsidian—a black, lustrous volcanic glass

conglomerate—a loosely cemented rock of pebbles and gravel

gneiss—a banded rock in which the minerals are arranged in layers

Instruct the students to write each heading on the appropriate lines and alphabetize each list of rocks under its heading.

Optional activity

Direct a writing activity—Review the difference between rocks and minerals. (See the Optional Activity in Lesson 8.) Tell the students that this activity is about rocks—specifically sedimentary rocks. Explain that one of the most fascinating features of sedimentary rocks is the fossils they sometimes contain. Direct each student to write a sentence or two explaining what Christians believe about the fossils in sedimentary rocks. *(During the Flood, layer after layer of material was deposited under the water. Many animals were trapped in these layers of deposited material, and fossils formed. Today we call these layers of deposited material containing fossils sedimentary rock.)*

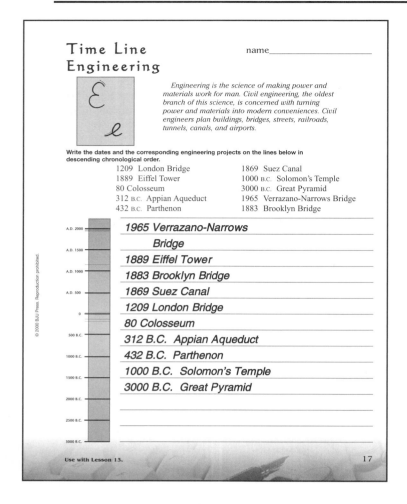

Materials and Preparation

Prepare:

- Handwriting lines on the chalkboard.

———— Lesson Content ————

Introduction

Lead a game—As you read the following descriptions, tell the students to guess the name of each of these structures.

1. This solid object has a flat base and four sides shaped like triangles that meet at the top. *(pyramid)*

2. This is a man-made body of water that connects two or more bodies of water. *(canal)*

3. This important structure is built across an obstacle so that people can cross to the other side of the obstacle. *(bridge)*

4. Used for public entertainment or assemblies, this is a large amphitheater. *(colosseum)*

5. This is a kind of building that is used for worship. *(temple)*

6. This can be a very tall building or a part of a tall building. *(tower)*

7. This pipe or channel is used to carry water a long distance. *(aqueduct)*

Direct attention to worktext page 17—Ask a student to read the description of civil engineering at the top of the page.

Skill development

Review the formation of *e*—Verbalize the direction of each stroke as you write the letters on the chalkboard. Point out that the uppercase letter begins at one o'clock and that the uppercase and lowercase *e* connect to letters that follow.

Begin at one,
Swing around toward three,
Swing around to five.

Swing up toward one and around to five.

Demonstrate the writing of lowercase *e* in pairs—Point out that the pencil is not lifted between letters. Tell the class to air-trace the letters, and then ask volunteers to write the following words on the chalkboard.

levees   *Greek*   *engineer*

Demonstrate alternate styles of writing the letter *e* (optional).

Guided practice

Guide the completion of worktext page 17—Ask students to read the list of engineering projects. Complete the time line together. Circulate among the students to make sure that they write the date and project on the correct line. Also check letter formation, alignment, and spacing.

26

Optional activity

Direct a writing activity—Tell the students to read about the building of Solomon's temple in I Kings 6:1-10. Help each student to figure out the size of the temple and its porch by converting the units of cubits to feet. Explain that to change cubits to feet, multiply by 1.5. Also explain that *threescore* means 3 times 20, or 60. Direct him to rewrite verses two and three on handwriting paper, using the answers he obtained in feet rather than in cubits. Then tell each student to write one sentence that describes each of the following parts of the temple.

1. windows *(Solomon made windows of narrow lights.)*
2. chambers *(He built chambers against the walls of the house round about.)*
3. house *(The house was built of stone covered with boards and beams of cedar.)*

(Other answers are acceptable.)

Lesson 14   A Geological Engineer   Worktext, page 18

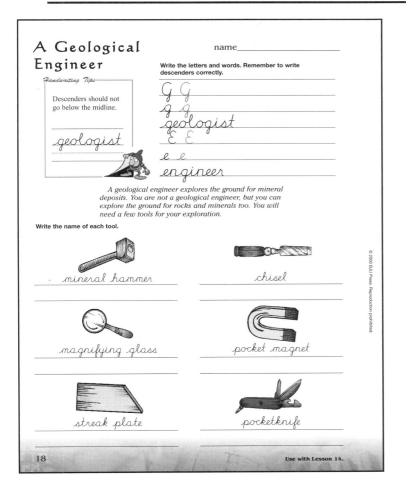

Materials and Preparation

Prepare:

- Two handwriting lines with a dotted midline on the chalkboard.
- The following sentence on the first handwriting line.

    George and Ed are geological engineers.

——— Lesson Content ———

Introduction

Create interest in today's lesson—Discuss the wide variety of jobs that a geologist can do. Ask how a geologist would make an important contribution to each situation listed below:

1. military programs *(make maps and air photos of certain regions)*
2. earth exploration *(locate deposits of oil, gas, precious stones, metals)*
3. ocean exploration *(locate deposits of oil, gas, sulphur)*
4. industry *(locate fuel sources)*
5. mining *(search for minerals and efficient ways to remove them)*

Skill development

Review the formation of *g* and *e*—Remind the students that the letters *g* and *e* connect to the letters that follow.

Focus on the handwriting tip on worktext page 18—Ask a student to read the handwriting tip aloud. Direct attention to the sentence on the chalkboard. Point out that the uppercase ascenders do not extend to the top line; they come within $\frac{1}{16}$" of the top line. Descenders extend to $\frac{3}{16}$" below the base line. Instruct a student to rewrite the sentence on the second handwriting line. Remind the student to avoid ascender-descender collision.

Guided practice

Focus on writing the letters *g* and *e*—Refer the students to the model letters and words at the top of worktext page 18. Instruct them to practice the letters and words on the lines provided.

Guide the completion of worktext page 18—Allow volunteers to read the paragraph and the name of each tool. Discuss the possible uses of each tool before instructing the students to complete the page.

Optional activity

Direct a writing activity—Review the fact that a geological engineer explores the ground for mineral deposits. Point out that this means that a geological engineer is concerned with the strength, permeability, and compactability of materials comprising the mineral deposits. Direct each student to look up the meaning of any of these terms that he does not know. Then direct him to write a sentence or two that tells why the geological engineer would want to know these qualities about the soil in connection with the selection of locations for large buildings, roads, railroads, bridges, dams, river and ocean piers, and harbor breakwaters. *(Each of these constructions depends on a solid foundation [strength]. They also depend on materials that do not allow much water to pass through [permeability] to erode the foundation. Finally, they depend on materials that do not pack or press together [compactability] so that they will not sink.)*

Lesson 15   **Bridge Building**   Worktext, page 19

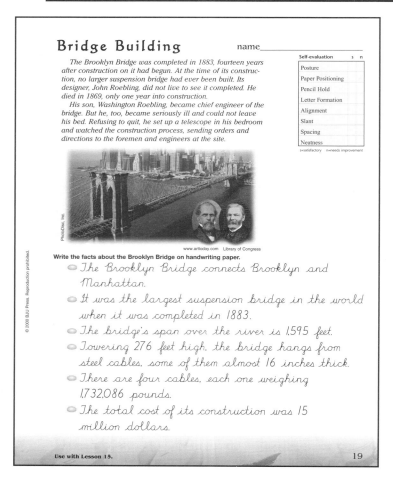

Materials and Preparation

Have available:

- Handwriting paper for each student.

Prepare:

- Handwriting lines on the chalkboard.

——— Lesson Content ———

Introduction

Relate the following information.

One of the most interesting kinds of bridges is the suspension bridge. It hangs on cables that are fastened to high towers. A long bridge of this type may have cables more than three feet thick, composed of thousands of twisted steel wires; but surprisingly, it costs less to build than an ordinary bridge. A suspension bridge is a beautiful sight, especially with the sun gleaming on its bright cables. If you've ever walked across a small suspension bridge and felt it wobble under your feet, you'll understand its one disadvantage: it tends to sway in the wind. The Mackinac Bridge connecting the two peninsulas of Michigan is a famous example of a suspension bridge. Another famous suspension bridge is the Brooklyn Bridge in New York.

Direct attention to worktext page 19—Ask a student to read the information about the Brooklyn Bridge at the top of the page.

Skill development

Review the formation of *g* and *e*—Choose several students to write the letters on the chalkboard as you verbalize the stroke descriptions. Ask how these uppercase letters are alike. *(They both begin at one o'clock and connect to letters that follow.)* Allow students to write the following statements on the chalkboard.

Dependability is the greatest ability.

Keep on keeping on.

Finish the job.

Assessment

Guide the completion of worktext page 19—Allow volunteers to read the directions and the facts about the Brooklyn Bridge. Encourage the students to do their best as they write the facts on handwriting paper. Remind them that after writing the facts they will evaluate their own handwriting on the chart.

You may want to use the evaluation form in the Appendix with this lesson. Be aware that the back of this page will be used in the next lesson on calligraphy.

Optional activity

Direct a writing activity—Relate the following information.

In his biography about Dr. Bob Jones Sr., R. K. Johnson called the evangelist a "Builder of Bridges" because Dr. Jones frequently quoted a poem entitled "Building the Bridge for Him." This poem tells about a different kind of bridge builder. It describes a person who "builds bridges" to others in order to lead them to Christ.

Direct each student to write a paragraph describing a way that he could "build a bridge" to an unsaved person that would point him to Christ.

Lesson 16   Calligraphy Letters *m* and *n*   Worktext, page 20

Materials and Preparation

Have available:

- A chisel-point pen for each student.
- A guide sheet for each student.
- A piece of typing paper for each student.
- A transparency of the lowercase guide sheet.
- An overhead projector.
- An overhead pen.

——— Lesson Content ———

Introduction

Review some of the terms listed on worktext page 104—Direct the students to turn to the Calligraphy Glossary on page 104 in their worktexts. Review the meaning of the terms related to the guide sheet. *(the slant lines, the x-height, and these two guidelines: base and body lines)* Then review the reason for using the guide sheet. *(to control the height and slant of each stroke)*

Skill development

Review some of the tips listed on worktext pages 105-6—Distribute the pen and a piece of typing paper to each student. Instruct him to lay these aside for later use. Direct attention to the Calligraphy Tips on pages 105-6 in the worktext. Read and demonstrate the tips about proper body position, paper position, and pen hold.

Read and demonstrate the tip about correct pen angle. Remind the students to draw a small box with a diagonal line from the top right corner to the bottom left corner to help them determine the 45° angle of the chisel point to the horizontal edge of the paper.

Review the instruction about breath control—Explain to the students that if they either hold their breath or breathe out when they write, they will have smoother-looking letters.

Review the practice strokes—Using the overhead pen, write the practice strokes on the lines on the overhead or white board.

Demonstrate the formation of lowercase *m* and *n*—Write the letters on the lines on the transparency, verbalizing the direction of each stroke as you write. Point out that both letters are made with one continuous stroke and that the curves are only on the tops of the letters. Point out to the students that the letters should not connect to the letters that follow.

29

Short diagonal right and drop,
Retrace and swing right,
Drop,
Retrace and swing right,
Drop and curve.

Short diagonal right and drop,
Retrace and swing right,
Drop and curve.

Demonstrate the spacing of letters within a word on worktext page 106—Direct the students to the Calligraphy Tips on page 106. Read and demonstrate tip 1 under spacing with the following examples.

1. Use the most space between two straight strokes in a word.

2. Use a little less space between a straight and a curved stroke.

3. Use the least space between two curved strokes.

Guided practice

Direct handwriting on worktext page 20—Review the calligraphy tip at the top of the page. Direct attention to the practice strokes. Then refer the students to the letter models on the lines at the bottom of the page. Remind them of the procedures for practicing the letters at the bottom of the page.

1. Note the arrow that indicates the direction of each stroke.
2. Trace the black letter with your finger.
3. Trace the gray letters with your pen.

Walk around the classroom to check that the students are making the correct strokes, both for practice strokes and for letter formations. Look for common errors.

> Refer to the Calligraphy Introduction on pages xxi-xxix.

Continued practice

Direct practice with typing paper and a guide sheet—Remind the students to use the side of the guide sheet labeled "Lowercase Guide Sheet." Tell them to write the practice strokes, new letters, and the letters that were taught in the previous calligraphy lessons (*c, a, o,* and *e*).

Write the word *ocean* on the overhead for the students to see. Tell them that this word will provide good review and practice in word formation. Be sure to collect the pens when the students have finished.

People and Professions

Inventor and Judge

The subject of inventors and their inventions is a fascinating one, especially to the creative mind of a child. On the other hand, some students may have never considered what a judge does, or God's role as judge in our lives. While reviewing the letters *i* and *j,* the class will examine the occupations of inventor and judge.

The last lesson in this unit is a calligraphy lesson and will require some advance preparation on your part. Please take time to practice the strokes required for introducing the new calligraphy letters.

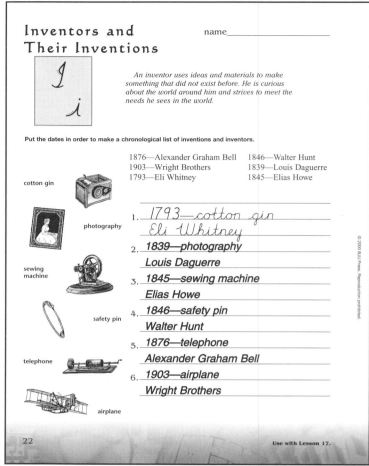

Inventors and
Their Inventions   name_____

An inventor uses ideas and materials to make something that did not exist before. He is curious about the world around him and strives to meet the needs he sees in the world.

Put the dates in order to make a chronological list of inventions and inventors.

1876—Alexander Graham Bell   1846—Walter Hunt
1903—Wright Brothers   1839—Louis Daguerre
1793—Eli Whitney   1845—Elias Howe

cotton gin

1. *1793—cotton gin*
   Eli Whitney

photography

2. *1839—photography*
   Louis Daguerre

sewing machine

3. *1845—sewing machine*
   Elias Howe

safety pin

4. *1846—safety pin*
   Walter Hunt

telephone

5. *1876—telephone*
   Alexander Graham Bell

6. *1903—airplane*
   Wright Brothers

airplane

22   Use with Lesson 17.

Materials and Preparation

Prepare:

- Handwriting lines on the chalkboard.

Lesson Content

Introduction

Introduce the unit—Direct attention to worktext page 21. Point out the two occupations to be studied in this unit: inventor and judge. Ask a student to read the unit verse. Choose students to respond to the following questions.

1. To whom does *he* refer in the verse? *(God)*

2. When will He come to judge the earth? *(Only He knows; at the end time.)*

3. What two kinds of judgment are there? *(for the saved—his works; for the unsaved—his unbelief)* Discuss personal implications as time permits. (BATs: 1b Repentance and faith; 4a Sowing and reaping)

Create interest in the lesson—Cite examples of well-known inventions *(the telegraph, the airplane, the telephone)* and ask the students to tell what their favorite inventions are. Direct attention to worktext page 22 and ask a student to read the information at the top of the page.

Skill development

Review the formation of *i*—Verbalize the direction of each stroke as you write the letters on the chalkboard. Remind the students that lowercase *i* is dotted after the entire word is written. Point out that uppercase *i* connects to letters that follow.

Swing around and up,
Drop and swing left,
Retrace and sweep up.

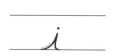

Swing up,
Drop low and curve,
Dot.

Demonstrate the writing of _i_—Tell the class to air-trace the letters, and then allow volunteers to write the following words on the chalkboard.

Indiana   invent   inventions

Demonstrate alternate styles of writing the letter _i_ (optional).

I T I

Guided practice

Guide the completion of worktext page 22—Encourage the students to write neatly as they complete the page independently.

Optional activity

Direct a writing activity—Relate the following information.

> The safety pin was invented in only three hours by Walter Hunt. He did this to pay a fifteen-dollar debt he owed to J. R. Chapin, a draftsman. Hunt not only discharged the debt he owed to Chapin but also earned a small sum as Chapin paid him four hundred dollars for all rights to the invention. Here is a small portion of the 1849 patent for the safety pin.

> Be it known that I, Walter Hunt, of the city, county, and State of New York, have invented a new and useful Improvement in the Make or Form of Dress-Pins, of which the following is a faithful and accurate description.

> The distinguishing features of this invention consist in the construction of a pin made of one piece of wire or metal combining a spring, and clasp or catch, in which catch, the point of said pin is forced and by its own spring securely retained. They may be made of common pin wire, or of the precious metals.

Direct each student to think of his own invention and then to write a patent for his invention.

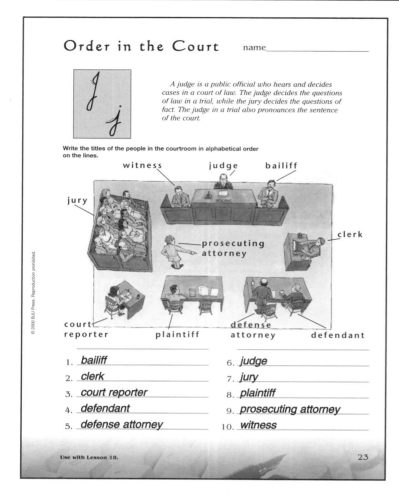

Order in the Court   name_____

A judge is a public official who hears and decides cases in a court of law. The judge decides the questions of law in a trial, while the jury decides the questions of fact. The judge in a trial also pronounces the sentence of the court.

Write the titles of the people in the courtroom in alphabetical order on the lines.

witness   judge   bailiff

jury

clerk

prosecuting attorney

court reporter   plaintiff   defense attorney   defendant

1. *bailiff*
2. *clerk*
3. *court reporter*
4. *defendant*
5. *defense attorney*
6. *judge*
7. *jury*
8. *plaintiff*
9. *prosecuting attorney*
10. *witness*

Use with Lesson 18.   23

Materials and Preparation

Prepare:

- Handwriting lines on the chalkboard.

——— Lesson Content ———

Introduction

Create interest in today's lesson—Tell the class to turn to page 23 in the worktext. Ask a student to read the paragraph at the top of the page. Instruct another student to read the titles of the people in the picture. Explain the function of each position represented.

1. clerk—keeps the records of the court
2. court reporter—records every word spoken at the trial

3. plaintiff—brings the complaint to the court
4. defendant—the person against whom the accusation is made
5. prosecuting attorney—represents the plaintiff
6. defense attorney—represents the defendant
7. witness—gives evidence at the trial
8. judge—hears and decides the case
9. bailiff—keeps order in the courtroom during the trial
10. jury—hears the evidence and gives a verdict

Skill development

Review the formation of *j*—Verbalize the direction of each stroke as you write the letters on the chalkboard. Remind the students that lowercase *j* is dotted after the entire word is written. Point out that both uppercase and lowercase *j* connect to letters that follow.

j

> ***Swing around and up,***
> ***Drop low and loop.***

j

> ***Swing up,***
> ***Drop low and loop,***
> ***Dot.***

Demonstrate the writing of the letter *j*—Tell the students to air-trace the letters, and then allow volunteers to write the following words on the chalkboard.

judicial   *justice*   *Judge Allen*

Demonstrate alternate styles of writing the letter *j* (optional).

Guided practice

Guide the completion of worktext page 23—Instruct the students to number the titles in the diagram in alphabetical order. Then direct them to complete the page independently.

Optional activity

Direct a writing activity—Make a copy of the following statements for each student. Ask the students to tell what they think a kangaroo court is. Then direct them to copy on handwriting paper the following statements of what different history books think a kangaroo court is.

1. An unauthorized or irregular court conducted with a disregard for legal rights and procedures; as a mock court held by prisoners in a jail, or an irregularly conducted court in a frontier district.

2. A term that arose in Kansas or Ohio to describe trials held by pioneer judges traveling (leaping) from place to place.

3. A later name for lynching trials, so named because the judges would fling themselves on the ground around the accused.

4. A mock trial held in a jail in 1870.

Lesson 19 Every Work into Judgment Worktext, page 24

Materials and Preparation

Have available:

- A Bible for each student.
- Handwriting paper for each student.

———— Lesson Content ————

Introduction

Direct a Bible study—Tell the students to turn in their Bibles to II Chronicles 26. After pointing out verse 1, which tells that Uzziah became king at sixteen years of age, ask a volunteer to read verses 9-15, the story of how Uzziah defended Jerusalem. Instruct the students to read verses 16-21 silently; then discuss God's judgment on Uzziah's pride. (BAT: 4a Sowing and reaping)

Skill development

Focus on the handwriting tip on worktext page 24—Remind the students that lowercase *i* and *j* are dotted after the entire word is written. Point out that both uppercase and lowercase *i* and *j* connect to letters that follow.

Guided practice

Focus on writing the letters *i* and *j*—Direct the students to the letters and words at the top of worktext page 24. Remind them to cross and dot the letters after writing each word on the lines provided.

Guide the completion of worktext page 24—Ask two students to read the verses. Instruct the students to use correct posture, paper positioning, and pencil hold as they write the verses on handwriting paper.

Optional activity

Direct a writing activity—Direct each student to read the account of God's judgment on the city of Babylon in Daniel chapter 5. Explain that in spite of man's efforts in building a strong city, God's will was done, and the Medes and Persians were able to take the city. Direct each student to write verses 25 through 28.

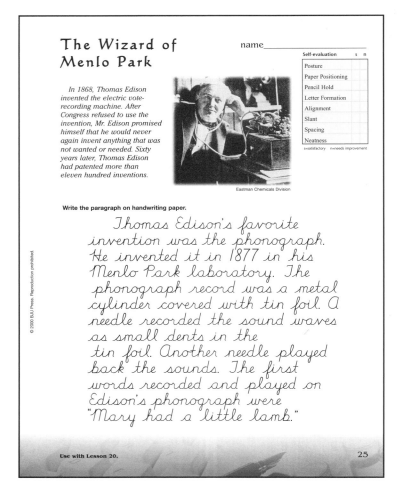

The Wizard of Menlo Park

name_____

Self-evaluation	s	n
Posture		
Paper Positioning		
Pencil Hold		
Letter Formation		
Alignment		
Slant		
Spacing		
Neatness		

s=satisfactory n=needs improvement

In 1868, Thomas Edison invented the electric vote-recording machine. After Congress refused to use the invention, Mr. Edison promised himself that he would never again invent anything that was not wanted or needed. Sixty years later, Thomas Edison had patented more than eleven hundred inventions.

Eastman Chemicals Division

Write the paragraph on handwriting paper.

Thomas Edison's favorite invention was the phonograph. He invented it in 1877 in his Menlo Park laboratory. The phonograph record was a metal cylinder covered with tin foil. A needle recorded the sound waves as small dents in the tin foil. Another needle played back the sounds. The first words recorded and played on Edison's phonograph were "Mary had a little lamb."

Use with Lesson 20.   25

Materials and Preparation

Have available:

- Handwriting paper for each student.

Prepare:

- Handwriting lines on the chalkboard.
- The following sentence on the chalkboard.

Thomas Edison patented more than eleven hundred inventions.

——— Lesson Content ———

Introduction

Introduce Thomas Edison—Read the following information to the students.

Thomas Edison, born in 1867, was a curious, questioning child who liked to experiment. He went to school when he was seven years old. He stayed there for only three months, irritating the teacher with his constant questions. His mother, who had once been a schoolteacher, decided to teach him at home. By the time he was twelve years old, Thomas had a job selling newspapers and snacks on a train. He printed his own newspaper in his spare time on the train and experimented with chemicals in the baggage car. Unfortunately, a stick of phosphorus burst into flames one day, setting the car on fire, and young Edison lost his job. He never gave up experimenting, however, and eventually became a famous inventor.

Direct attention to worktext page 25—Ask a student to read the information at the top of the page.

Skill development

Review the formation of *i* and *j*—Allow several students to write the letters on the chalkboard as you verbalize each stroke. Remind the students that lowercase *i* and *j* are dotted after the entire word is written. Ask how the uppercase and lowercase letters are alike. *(They all connect to letters that follow them.)*

Review the components on the self-evaluation chart.

posture	alignment
paper positioning	slant
pencil hold	spacing
letter formation	neatness

Direct attention to the sentence written on the chalkboard—Point out the most common errors in alignment, slant, and spacing.

Review the indention of paragraphs—Point out that paragraphs are indented to set them apart from the rest of the reading material and to make them easier to read.

Assessment

Guide the completion of worktext page 25—Direct a student to read the instructions and the paragraph about the phonograph. Instruct the students to complete the page independently.

You may want to use the evaluation form in the Appendix with this lesson. Be aware that the back of this page will be used in the next lesson on calligraphy.

Optional activity

Direct a writing activity—Read the following paragraph about the phonograph to the students and allow them to give the answers to complete the statements. As the students give the answers, write each one on the chalkboard. Then direct the students to write the list on handwriting paper.

Sounds are caused by back-and-forth movements called *(vibrations)*. When *(Thomas Edison)* invented the phonograph in 1877, he was aware of this fact. His phonograph consisted of a cylinder with grooves etched on its surface and a stylus. The *(grooves)* on the cylinder varied in depth so that when the cylinder was rotated and the *(stylus)* ran in the groove, the *(stylus)* moved up and down. This vibration of the stylus produced the *(sound)*.

Lesson 21   Calligraphy Letters *v* and *w*   Worktext, page 26

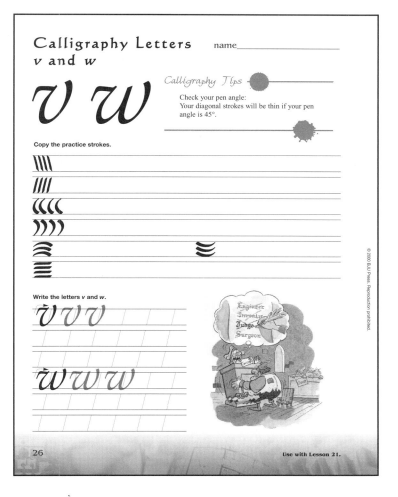

Lesson Content

Introduction

Review some of the information relating to the guide sheet—Choose a student to demonstrate the terms relating to the guide sheet. *(the slant lines, the x-height, and these two guidelines: the base and body lines)* Ask another student to explain the reason for using the guide sheet. *(to control the height and slant of each stroke)*

Skill development

Review some of the terms listed in the Calligraphy Glossary—Ask a student to demonstrate the proper body position, paper position, and pen hold. Ask another student to demonstrate the correct pen angle.

Review the instruction about breath control—Explain to the students that if they either hold their breath or breathe out when they write, they will have smoother-looking letters.

Review the practice strokes—Ask a student to come to the overhead or white board and demonstrate the practice strokes. You may need to help him.

Demonstrate the formation of lowercase *v* and *w*—Write the letters on the lines on the transparency, verbalizing the direction of each stroke as you write. Point out that both letters are made with one continuous stroke and that the curves are only on the bottoms of the letters. Remind the students that the letters should not connect to the letters that follow them.

Materials and Preparation

Have available:

- A chisel-point pen for each student.
- A guide sheet for each student.
- A piece of typing paper for each student.
- A transparency of the lowercase guide sheet.
- An overhead projector.
- An overhead pen.

Short stroke up,
Glide right,
Drop and swing around
   and up above body line.

 Short stroke up,
Glide right,
Drop and swing around
 and up to body line,
Retrace and swing around
 and up above body line.

students to the letter models on the lines at the bottom of the page. Remind them of the procedures for practicing the letters at the bottom of the page.

1. Note the arrow that indicates the direction of each stroke.
2. Trace the black letter with your finger.
3. Trace the gray letters with your pen.

Walk around the classroom to check that the students are making the correct strokes, both for practice strokes and for letter formation. Look for common errors.

Review the rules for spacing within a word—Direct the students to the Calligraphy Tips on worktext page 106. Review the three parts of the rule for spacing within a work.

Continued practice

Direct practice with typing paper and a guide sheet—Remind the students to use the side of the guide sheet labeled "Lowercase Guide Sheet." Tell each student to write the practice strokes, new letters, and the letters that were taught in the previous calligraphy lessons *(c, a, o, e, m,* and *n).*

 See Calligraphy Tips on worktext pages 105-6.

Write the words *vow* and *ocean* on the overhead. Tell the students that both words will provide good review and practice in word formation. Be sure to collect the pens when the students have finished.

Guided practice

Direct handwriting on worktext page 26—Direct the students to set the guide sheet and typing paper aside for practice later. Review the calligraphy tip at the top of the page. Direct attention to the practice strokes. Then refer the

People and Professions

Surgeon and Dentist

In this unit the students will review letters *s* and *d* while they consider the work of the surgeon and the dentist. Many sixth-graders view surgeons and dentists with a combination of curiosity and fear. Learning about them often helps to give students a more objective viewpoint.

Remember to prepare now for the calligraphy lesson at the end of the unit. You will become more skilled at making the new strokes as you practice faithfully.

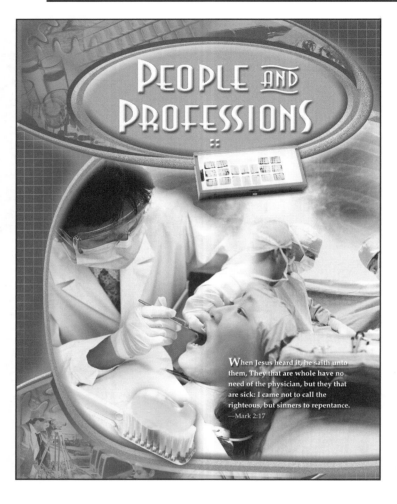

The following appears in the worktext page shown:

Word "Searchery"   name_____

Surgeons treat disease and injury by operating on the affected parts of a person's body. A surgeon never operates alone but is part of a surgical team that includes a first assistant, an anesthesiologist, and a nurse.

Circle the surgeon's supplies and the anesthesiologist's supplies. On handwriting paper, write the surgeon's supplies in one column and the anesthesiologist's supplies in another column.

DOWN—Surgeon's Supplies

scissors   clamps
scalpels   needles
sponges   sutures

ACROSS—Anesthesiologist's Supplies

anesthetics   oxygen
drugs   stethoscope
masks   syringes

A	C	S	T	E	T	H	O	S	C	O	P	E	A	E	I
E	I	U	K	Q	S	Y	B	P	F	J	N	R	V	Z	S
G	T	T	S	Q	U	Y	F	O	X	Y	G	E	N	H	G
M	X	U	C	P	V	X	Z	N	A	S	K	B	E	Z	E
S	Y	R	I	N	G	E	S	G	X	P	H	T	E	X	C
O	C	E	S	K	M	L	C	E	W	D	G	L	D	V	L
I	G	S	S	O	Q	M	A	S	K	S	O	K	L	T	A
W	K	O	O	E	G	C	L	Z	T	I	C	M	E	R	M
D	O	J	R	Y	V	U	P	H	R	V	Q	S	S	P	P
J	S	L	S	R	A	N	E	S	T	H	E	T	I	C	S
L	W	R	J	O	N	M	L	J	I	F	E	B	A	N	C
P	S	F	D	R	U	G	S	O	B	Y	W	U	S	Q	A

Materials and Preparation

Prepare:

- Handwriting lines on the chalkboard.

——— Lesson Content ———

Introduction

Introduce the unit—Direct attention to worktext page 27. Explain that this unit discusses some interesting facts about surgeons and dentists. Ask a student to read the unit verse.

Relate the following information.

One thing that a surgeon has to be very careful about is keeping germs from infecting his patient during and after an operation. Years ago, many patients in hospitals died because of infection. In 1865 Joseph Lister introduced the use of antiseptics, thereby saving the lives of hundreds of people. Surgeons today make sure that every piece of equipment used in an operation is sterile, including their hands, so that there will be no danger of infection.

Direct attention to worktext page 28—Ask a student to read the information at the top of the page.

Skill development

Review the formation of *s*—Verbalize the direction of each stroke as you write the letters on the chalkboard. Point out that the letter *s* connects to letters that follow.

Swing up,
Curve left and loop,
Swing around to lock,
Sweep out.

Swing up,
Then down and around to
*   lock,*
Sweep out.

Demonstrate the writing of the letter *s*—Tell the students to air-trace the letters, and then allow volunteers to write the following words on the chalkboard.

sutures   *stethoscope*   *sponges*

Demonstrate the writing of lowercase *s* in pairs—Point out that the pencil is not lifted between letters. Tell the class to air-trace the letters, and then allow several volunteers to write the following words on the chalkboard.

scissors   *witness*   *Russia*

Demonstrate alternate styles of writing the letter *s* (optional).

Guided practice

Guide the completion of worktext page 28—Ask a volunteer to read the instructions. Tell the students to complete the page independently.

Optional activity

Direct a writing activity—Direct each student to write the following surgery discoveries in the order that he thinks the discoveries occurred. Then give the students the correct order as indicated by the numbers in the parentheses.

(4) x-rays
(2) identification of micro-organisms as the cause of infection in wounds
(1) ether anesthesia
(5) blood typing
(3) antiseptics

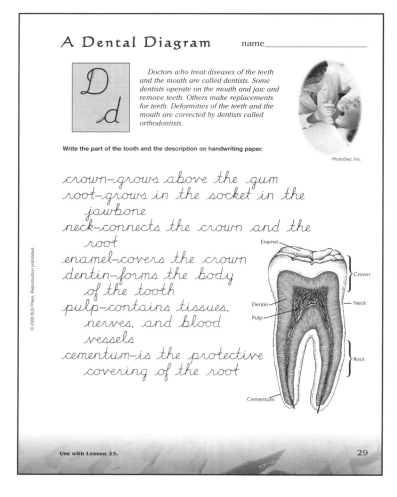

A Dental Diagram   name_____

Doctors who treat diseases of the teeth and the mouth are called dentists. Some dentists operate on the mouth and jaw and remove teeth. Others make replacements for teeth. Deformities of the teeth and the mouth are corrected by dentists called orthodontists.

PhotoDisc, Inc.

Write the part of the tooth and the description on handwriting paper.

crown—grows above the gum
root—grows in the socket in the
    jawbone
neck—connects the crown and the
    root
enamel—covers the crown
dentin—forms the body
    of the tooth
pulp—contains tissues,
    nerves, and blood
    vessels
cementum—is the protective
    covering of the root

Enamel / Crown / Dentin / Pulp / Neck / Root / Cementum

Use with Lesson 23.   29

© 2000 BJU Press. Reproduction prohibited.

Materials and Preparation

Prepare:

- Handwriting lines on the chalkboard.

———— Lesson Content ————

Introduction

Direct a spelling bee—Divide the class into two teams. Have the two teams line up at the chalkboard. Call out the following words one at a time.

cavity	*enamel*	*painless*
x-ray	*braces*	*anesthetic*
prevention	*extraction*	*deformity*
orthodontics	*filling*	*dentistry*

Direct the first team members in each line to write the word on the chalkboard. The first to spell the word correctly wins a point for his team. The team with the most points at the end of the spelling bee wins.

Direct attention to worktext page 29—Ask a student to read the information at the top of the page.

Skill development

Review the formation of *d*—Verbalize the direction of each stroke as you write the letters on the chalkboard. Point out that the uppercase *d* does not connect to letters that follow but that lowercase *d* does.

Drop low and loop left,
Swing around and over to
    lock.

Swing up and around to
    one,
Retrace and swing around
    and up,
Climb high,
Retrace and curve.

Demonstrate the writing of lowercase *d* in pairs—Point out that the pencil is not lifted between letters. Tell the class to air-trace the letters, and then allow several volunteers to write the following words on the chalkboard.

    shredded   *meddle*   *reddish*   *ladder*

Demonstrate alternate styles of writing the letter *d* (optional).

Guided practice

Guide the completion of worktext page 29—Instruct the students to locate the seven parts of the tooth on the diagram as volunteers read the seven words and their definitions. Check letter formation, slant, alignment, and overall neatness as the students write the phrases that describe the parts of the teeth.

Optional activity

Direct a writing activity—Prepare a copy of the following lists of dental firsts. Instruct each student to choose one interesting fact and to write it on handwriting paper.

1. In his book written in 1728, Pierre Fauchard described the first dental drill as a hand-held drill operated by twisting it in alternate directions.

2. The first dental practitioner in Britain was Peter de la Roche. He practiced in London in 1661.

3. An edict of Louis XIV in 1699 was the first list of professional qualifications for dental practitioners.

4. The earliest known set of dentures composed of both upper and lower rows of false teeth is believed to date from the late 1400s. They are composed of teeth carved from bone attached to hinged side-pieces with gut.

Direct an art activity—Direct each student to design and make his own toothpaste box. Encourage him to use his best handwriting when writing the name of the toothpaste and its contents on the box.

Lesson 24　　Signs of the Time　　Worktext, page 30

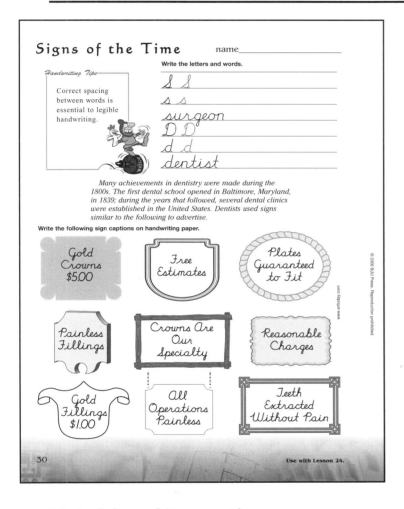

Materials and Preparation

Have available:

- Handwriting paper for each student.

Prepare:

- Handwriting lines on the chalkboard.
- The following words on the chalkboard.

quarrier	geologist
civil engineer	judge
oceanographer	inventor
calligrapher	astronomer

——— Lesson Content ———

Introduction

Play a review game—As you read the words below, tell the students to match each one with an occupation listed on the chalkboard.

> swash *(calligrapher)*; refractor *(astronomer)*; tides *(oceanographer)*; feathers *(quarrier)*; streak plate *(geologist)*; pyramid *(civil engineer)*; bailiff *(judge)*; telephone *(inventor)*.

To make it a more challenging game, put the clue words on the chalkboard instead of the occupation and have the class guess which occupation they match.

Direct attention to worktext page 30—Ask a student to read the paragraph about dentistry.

Skill development

Focus on the handwriting tip on worktext page 30—Point out the handwriting tip at the top of the page. Dictate the following sentences and allow several students to write them on the chalkboard.

> *Dr. Smith is a surgeon.*
> *My dentist's name is Dr. Darry.*

Remind the students to use correct spacing.

Guided practice

Focus on writing the letters *s* and *d*—Direct the students to write the letters and words at the top of worktext page 30.

Guide the completion of worktext page 30—Instruct the students to complete the page independently.

Optional activity

Complete a poem—Provide a copy of the following poem for each student. Direct him to write on handwriting paper a final verse to complete the poem.

As I was walking down the street
  A billboard met my eye.
The advertisement posted there
  Would make one laugh and cry.

It rained and hailed the other night
  And washed it half away.
The other half remaining there
  Would make this billboard say:

Lesson 25   The Great Physician   Worktext, page 31

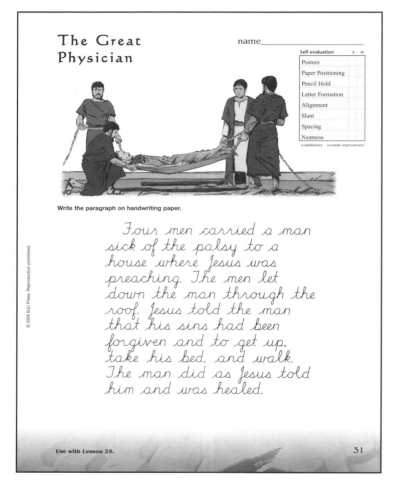

Materials and Preparation

Have available:

- Handwriting paper for each student.

Prepare:

- Handwriting lines on the chalkboard.
- The following words on the chalkboard.

scalpel	x-ray	stethoscope
mask	retractor	gloves
sutures	sphygmomanometer	

Lesson Content

Introduction

Create interest with a game—Tell the class that today they must take a test in order to see if they are qualified to enter a famous medical college. (Insert the name of a local medical school if you have one in your area.) As you read the definitions below, ask the students to match them with the list of surgical equipment on the chalkboard.

1. This is used to listen to sounds produced by the heart. *(stethoscope)*
2. This allows the surgeon to breathe without contaminating the patient. *(mask)*
3. These are made of thread and are used to close an open wound. *(sutures)*
4. This is a small knife with a thin, sharp blade. *(scalpel)*
5. This is an important tool for diagnosis. *(x-ray)*
6. This instrument holds back the edges of a wound. *(retractor)*
7. These help keep the surgeon's hands sterile. *(gloves)*
8. This instrument measures blood pressure. *(sphygmomanometer)*

Direct attention to worktext page 31—Comment that Jesus, the Great Physician, healed His patients perfectly and did not need the complicated equipment that doctors use today.

Skill development

Review the formation of *s* and *d*—Allow several students to write the letters on the chalkboard as you verbalize each stroke. Ask how these lowercase letters are alike. *(They connect to letters that follow.)* Ask how the uppercase letters *s* and *d* are different. *(Uppercase* s *connects to letters that follow; uppercase* d *does not.)*

Review alignment and spacing—Write the word *alignment* on the chalkboard. Explain that each letter should rest on the base line; each ascender (tall letter) should extend from the base line to within ¹⁄₁₆" of the top line. Point out that the tall letters need to be the same height. The short letters also need to be the same height, touching the

44

imaginary mid-line. Emphasize that correct spacing is essential for neat, legible writing. Students should leave approximately ⅛" of space between each word.

Assessment

Guide the completion of worktext page 31—Direct a student to read the paragraph. Discuss the criteria for the self-evaluation, and then instruct the students to write the paragraph neatly on handwriting paper.

 You may want to use the evaluation form in the Appendix with this lesson. Be aware that the back of this page will be used in the next lesson on calligraphy.

Optional activities

Direct a Bible study—Give the following information to the students.

A physician can be defined as one who practices the healing art—including medicine and surgery. He practices medicine in the sense that he uses preparations (medicines) to treat diseases, and surgery in the sense that he operates or uses manual (with the hand) procedures to treat disease. The Scripture does not mention the surgical aspect of a physician, but it does mention the medicinal aspect.

Direct each student to look up the following Bible references and to write the name of the substance used as a medicine beside its reference.

Genesis 37:25 *(balm)*
Isaiah 1:6 *(ointment)*
Jeremiah 51:8 *(balm)*
II Kings 20:7 *(lump of figs, i.e., a plaster poultice)*
Luke 10:34 *(oil and wine)*

Next direct each student to look up the following references and to write the name of the disease known in biblical times beside its reference.

Deuteronomy 28:28 *(blindness)*
Job 2:7 *(boils)*
Exodus 9:9 *(blains—a swelling)*
II Timothy 2:17 *(canker—a consumption, gangrene)*
Mark 5:25 *(issue—to run with blood)*

Direct a Bible study—Read Song of Solomon 1:3 to the students. Point out the portion that says "Thy name (referring to Christ) is as ointment poured forth." Tell them that the Scripture has many things to say about ointment, and in looking at some of these references we can find out some things about Christ's name and therefore about Christ Himself. Write the following Bible references on the chalkboard; then mix up the order of the statements about ointment and give a copy of them to each student. Direct each student to look up the verses and to write the references next to the statement that they apply to. You may want to use the information following each statement for discussion.

John 12:3—Ointment was very costly; and when poured forth, it filled the house with its odor. *(Christ is our precious Savior; and when His blood was poured forth, it was as a sweet-smelling sacrifice to God in heaven.)*

Exodus 30:35-36—Ointment was beaten to make a perfume. *(See the explanation for John 12:3.)*

Exodus 30:25-27—Holy ointment was used to purify the instruments in the temple. *(It is through Christ that we are made pure.)*

Exodus 30:30—Holy ointment was used to anoint priests. *(In I Peter 2:9 we are called "a chosen generation, a royal priesthood." Because of Christ's sufferings on the cross—like the beaten ointment—we are anointed as royal priests.)*

Skill development

Review some of the terms listed in the Calligraphy Glossary—Ask a student to demonstrate the proper body position, paper position, and pen hold. Ask another student to demonstrate the correct pen angle.

Review the instruction about breath control—Explain to the students that if they either hold their breath or breathe out when they write, they will have smoother-looking letters.

Review the practice strokes—Ask a student to come to the overhead or white board and demonstrate the practice strokes. You may need to help him.

Demonstrate the formation of lowercase *u, i,* and *r*—Write the letters on the lines on the transparency, verbalizing the direction of each stroke as you write. Remind the students that these letters should not connect to other letters that follow. Point out that the *u* is basically an upside down *n,* the *r* is a short-legged *n,* and the *i* is the same basic stroke as the first part of *n.*

Short diagonal right,
Drop and swing right,
Push up to the body line,
Retrace and curve.

Materials and Preparation

Have available:

- A chisel-point pen for each student.
- A guide sheet for each student.
- A piece of typing paper for each student.
- A transparency of the lowercase guide sheet.
- An overhead projector.
- An overhead pen.

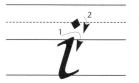

(1) Short diagonal right,
  Drop and curve.
(2) Dot.

——— Lesson Content ———

Introduction

Review some of the information relating to the guide sheet—Choose a student to demonstrate the terms relating to the guide sheet. *(the slant lines, the x-height, and these two guidelines: the base and body lines)* Ask another student to explain the reason for using the guide sheet. *(to control the height and slant of each stroke)*

Short diagonal right and
  drop,
Retrace and swing right.

Guided practice

Direct handwriting on worktext page 32—Review the calligraphy tip at the top of the page. Direct attention to the practice strokes. Then refer the students to the letter models on the lines at the bottom of the page. Remind them of the procedures for practicing the letters at the bottom of the page.

1. Note the arrow that indicates the direction of each stroke.
2. Trace the black letter with your finger.
3. Trace the gray letters with your pen.

Walk around the classroom to check that the students are making the correct strokes, both for practice strokes and for letter formation. Look for common errors.

Continued practice

Direct practice with typing paper and a guide sheet—Remind the students to use the side of the guide sheet labeled "Lowercase Guide Sheet." Tell each student to write the practice strokes, new letters, and the letters that were taught in the previous lessons *(c, a, o, e, m, n, v,* and *w)*. Write the word *crime* on the overhead for the students to see. Point out that this word will provide good review and practice in word formation. Be sure to collect the pens when the students have finished.

People and Professions

Tailor and Fisherman

The letters *t* and *f,* which have similar beginning strokes, are reviewed in this unit; the corresponding occupations are tailor and fisherman. The students will have a chance to do some creative thinking during the activities in these lessons.

Please read the entire unit, paying particular attention to the calligraphy lesson. Allow yourself plenty of time to practice new strokes before teaching the calligraphy letters.

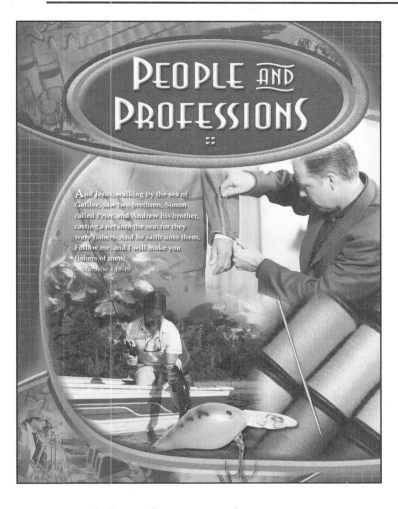

Sew—Sew   name_____

Tailors make, repair, and alter clothing. Most tailors measure customers, fit or make patterns, and then sew garments. Once tailoring was a common profession; but with the invention of sewing machines and mass production of clothing, it has decreased in popularity. However, some people still earn their living making hand-tailored clothes.

A tailor uses many sewing tools. Write the names of the tools on the handwriting lines.

sewing machine
needles
thimble
tape measure
pins
iron
thread
scissors

Tailors must also use fastenings on the garments they make. Write the name of the fastener below each picture.

button   hook and eye   zipper   snap

34   Use with Lesson 27.

© 2000 BJU Press. Reproduction prohibited.

Materials and Preparation

Have available:

- A dress or suit pattern with its instruction sheet.

Prepare:

- Handwriting lines on the chalkboard.

——— Lesson Content ———

Introduction

Introduce the unit—Direct attention to worktext page 33 and ask what occupations are represented. If anyone seems unsure of what a tailor does, explain that he makes and repairs clothes. Ask a student to read the unit verse aloud and tell what Jesus meant by saying that He would make them fishers of men. *(They would win men to Him.)* Ask the class if they can think of one characteristic that tailors and fishermen and soulwinners need. *(Answers will vary but may include patience.)*

Display the pattern and instruction sheet—Point out to the class that the pattern looks complicated unless you know what to do with it. Explain that a dress (or a suit) is hard to complete successfully without referring to the instruction sheet. Add any anecdotes from your personal sewing experiences that apply. Remind the students that God has a plan or a pattern for our lives. Mention that it is sometimes hard to trust that His plan will work out well and that we need to read our instructions in the Bible. (BAT: 6a Bible study)

Direct attention to worktext page 34—Ask a student to read the information at the top of the page.

Skill development

Review the formation of *t*—Verbalize the direction of each stroke as you write the letters on the chalkboard. Remind the students that lowercase *t* is crossed after the entire word is written. Point out that uppercase *t* does not connect to letters that follow but that lowercase *t* does.

Swing over and up,
Drop and swing left.

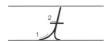

(1) Swing up,
    Retrace and curve right.
(2) Cross.

Demonstrate the writing of lowercase *t* in pairs—Point out that the pencil is not lifted between letters. Tell the class to air-trace the letters, and then allow volunteers to write the following words on the chalkboard.

    written   *tatter*   *button*   *mitt*

Demonstrate alternate styles of writing the letter *t* (optional).

Guided practice

Guide the completion of worktext page 34—Ask a volunteer to read the instructions. Direct the students to complete the page using their best cursive writing.

Optional activity

Direct a writing activity—Direct each student to look up the following verses about sewing. Ask him to write the name of the item being sewn next to each reference.

    Genesis 3:7 *(fig leaves)*
    Exodus 36:37 *(hanging for the tabernacle)*
    Acts 18:3 *(tents)*

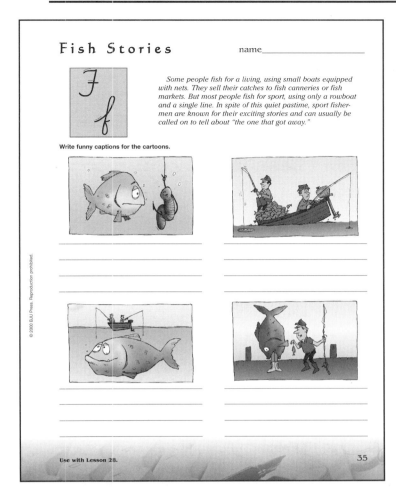

letters that follow but that lowercase *f* does. Point out the words on the chalkboard.

**(1) Swing over and up,
Drop and swing left.
(2) Cross.**

**Swing up,
Curve left and drop low,
Curve right and up to lock,
Bounce.**

Demonstrate the writing of lowercase *f* in pairs—Point out that the pencil is not lifted between letters. Write the following words on the chalkboard.

staff   *traffic*   *fluff*

Allow several students to write them, using your examples as models.

Demonstrate alternate styles of writing the letter *f* (optional).

Guided practice

Guide the completion of worktext page 35—Elicit several possible captions for the cartoons and write them on the chalkboard. Check paper position, pencil hold, and posture as students write original captions.

Optional activity

Direct a writing activity—Give the following information to the students.

> Fish have been important to man since the early times. In fact, the symbol of Christianity for two hundred years after Christ's ascension was the fish. The Greek word for "fish" was used as an acrostic; that is, each letter in the word *fish* stood for a word in the Greek phrase—*Jesus Christ God's Son Savior*. The Christians continued to use the fish as a symbol for Christianity until crucifixion became illegal in the Roman Empire; then they used the cross.

Write the following Bible references on the chalkboard. Instruct each student to look up these references of fish stories. Direct him to write on handwriting paper the characters involved in each story next to its reference.

Materials and Preparation

Prepare:
- Handwriting lines on the chalkboard.
- The following words on the chalkboard.

Fred   *fisherman*

——— Lesson Content ———

Introduction

Lead a discussion—Instruct the students to turn to worktext page 35. Ask them to read the paragraph at the top of the page silently and to think of any interesting fishing experiences they have had. Allow several students to tell their fishing stories.

Skill development

Review the formation of *f*—Verbalize the direction of each stroke as you write the letters on the chalkboard. Remind the students that uppercase *f* is crossed after the entire word is written. Point out that uppercase *f* does not connect to the

Matthew 14:15-21 *(five thousand men, women, and children; the disciples; Christ)*

Matthew 15:32-39 *(four thousand men, women, and children; the disciples; Christ)*

Matthew 17:24-27 *(the tribute collectors, Peter, Christ)*

Luke 5:4-11 *(Simon Peter, James and John, the fishermen in the other boat, Christ)*

John 21:1-14 *(Simon Peter, Thomas, Nathanael, the sons of Zebedee [James and John], two other disciples, Christ)*

Lesson 29   Seven at One Blow   Worktext, page 36

Seven at One Blow   name_____

Write the letters and words.

Handwriting Tips

Margins are imaginary lines on both sides of your paper.

J J
t t
tailor
F F
f f
fisherman

© 2000 BJU Press. Reproduction prohibited.

Write the sentences in sequential order on handwriting paper.

6 ◯ The clever tailor caused a fight to start between two giants.
2 ◯ The tailor sewed the words "seven at one blow" on his belt.
4 ◯ Two giants beat the tailor's bed.
3 ◯ The giant squeezed water out of a rock.
1 ◯ The tailor killed seven flies at one blow.
7 ◯ The king's daughter and the tailor married and lived happily ever after.
5 ◯ The king told the tailor to prove his bravery by killing the giants.

36   Use with Lesson 29.

Materials and Preparation

Prepare:

- The following words on the chalkboard.

mousetrap	gun
book	plate
spoon	button
pop-up tissues	paper clip

——— Lesson Content ———

Introduction

Create interest in the lesson.

Part of today's lesson is a story you may recognize. It is about a tailor who made rather grand claims about what he could do. In advertisements today, you often hear exaggerated and flowery language used to describe a product. The purpose, of course, is to make you want to buy that product. Can you tell which of the items listed on the chalkboard are described by these sentences?

1. This is an ingenious device of steel and hardwood that is guaranteed to rid your household of unwanted intruders. *(mousetrap)*

2. This tiny, silver-colored implement performs the valuable task of keeping your papers in order. *(paper clip)*

3. There are a hundred uses for these soft, pliable layers of paper that emerge from their container at a flick of your hand. *(pop-up tissues)*

4. This is a most useful object that comes in a variety of sizes, shapes, and colors. It is found in elevators, on shirts, and is used to describe noses. *(button)*

Skill development

Focus on the handwriting tip on worktext page 36—Call attention to the handwriting tip at the top of the page. Direct the students to leave a margin on both sides of their papers.

Guided practice

Focus on writing the letter *t* and *f*—Call attention to the model letters at the top of worktext page 36. Remind the students that lowercase *t* and uppercase *f* are crossed after the entire word is written. Point out that lowercase *t* and *f* connect to letters that follow but that uppercase *t* and *f* do not. Instruct the students to write the letters and words on the lines provided.

Discuss a fairy tale—Ask the students if anyone has heard the story of "The Brave Little Tailor." If someone knows the story, allow him to tell it. If not, relate the following story to the students. Explain that this is from *Grimm's Fairy Tales*.

One morning a little tailor was stitching merrily in his shop. On his table was a piece of bread covered with delicious jam. The jam was so sweet that soon a great many flies were attracted to it. The tailor shooed them away, but they came back in only greater number. Finally, he grabbed a flyswatter and swung it back and forth. When he stopped, seven flies lay dead. "Seven at one blow," said the tailor and quickly sewed himself a belt with the words "seven at one blow" embroidered on it. Then he went out to see the world.

He soon encountered a giant who was impressed with the tailor's bravery (though, of course, he thought the "seven at one blow" meant men and not flies). To test the tailor, he squeezed water out of a rock and challenged the tailor to do the same. The tailor tricked the giant by squeezing the whey out of a piece of old cheese that he had brought with him.

The giant invited the tailor to spend the night in a cave with other giants. The bed, however, was so big that the tailor crawled up in the corner of the room to sleep instead. During the night the giant came in and beat the bed, thinking he was killing the tailor. When the giants saw the tailor the next day, they thought he was a spirit and ran away.

The tailor continued on his merry way until he came to the palace. The king and all his court were amazed at the tailor's great claim. The king promised the tailor his daughter in marriage and half the kingdom if he could rid the land of two giants that were continually bothering his realm.

"Just the thing for someone brave like me," said the tailor, and he set out. In the woods he spied the two giants lying asleep under a tree. He filled his pockets with stones and climbed to a branch over the giants. The tailor threw a stone down and hit one of the giants.

The giant woke up and asked his companion why he had hit him. Of course the second giant denied hitting the first. Soon they were both asleep again. The tailor hit the second giant with a stone. When he awoke, he accused the first giant of hitting him. Soon they were fighting and beating up on each other until they were both quite dead.

The little tailor went back to the king and claimed his prize. He married the princess, and they lived happily ever after.

Guide the completion of worktext page 36—Help the students to put the sentences in the correct order. Remind them to leave a margin on both sides of their papers as they write the sentences in sequential order.

Optional activity

Direct a listening activity—Read "The Emperor's New Clothes" to the students. Direct each student to write on handwriting paper the moral of the story.

There Were Twelve Disciples

name_____

Before they became fishers of men, some of Jesus' disciples fished along the Sea of Galilee. When Jesus called Simon Peter and Andrew, they were at work fishing in the sea. James and John, the sons of Zebedee, were mending their nets when Jesus called them to follow Him. These men left everything behind to follow and live with Christ.

Self-evaluation	s	n
Posture		
Paper Positioning		
Pencil Hold		
Letter Formation		
Alignment		
Slant		
Spacing		
Neatness		

s=satisfactory   n=needs improvement

Write the names of Jesus' disciples on the lines.

Simon Peter
Andrew
James
John
Philip
Thomas
Matthew
James
Thaddeus
Simon
Judas Iscariot
Bartholomew

Write the names of the four disciples who were fishermen.

Simon Peter	James
John	Andrew

Use with Lesson 30.   37

3. The fisherman throws in a baited hook and waits for a bite. *(still fishing)*

4. A moving boat tows the bait or lure. *(trolling)*

Direct attention to worktext page 37—Ask a student to read the paragraph about the disciples.

Skill development

Review the formation of *t* and *f*—Direct several students to write the letters on the chalkboard as you verbalize the stroke descriptions. Ask how these uppercase letters are alike. *(They do not connect to letters that follow.)* Point out that these lowercase letters connect to letters that follow. Remind the students that uppercase *f* and lowercase *t* are not crossed until the entire word is written. Allow volunteers to write the following verse phrases on the chalkboard.

> *Follow me.*
>
> *Be ye therefore followers of God.*
>
> *Teach me thy paths.*

Assessment

Guide the completion of worktext page 37—Instruct a student to read the directions. Direct the students to complete the page independently.

You may want to use the evaluation form in the Appendix with this lesson. Be aware that the back of this page will be used in the next lesson on calligraphy.

Optional activity

Direct a writing activity—Direct the students to look up the following references and to write on handwriting paper the fishing method mentioned next to its reference.

> Mark 1:16 *(netting)*
> Isaiah 19:8 *(angling with a hook and netting)*
> Ezekiel 26:5 *(netting)*
> Habakkuk 1:15 *(angling with a hook, netting, and dragging)*
> Matthew 4:18 *(netting)*

Materials and Preparation

Prepare:

- The following words on the chalkboard.

  still fishing   *trolling*

  casting   *ice fishing*

- Handwriting lines on the chalkboard.

—— Lesson Content ——

Introduction

Lead a guessing game—Direct the students' attention to the words on the chalkboard. Tell them to guess the different methods of fishing as you read the following clues.

1. A fish is pulled in by cranking a reel handle. *(casting)*

2. A tip-up device signals that a fish is caught. *(ice fishing)*

Calligraphy
Letters *s* and *t*

s t

name_____

Calligraphy Tips
Leave a space of an "o" between words.

Copy the practice strokes.

Write the letters *s* and *t*.

s s s

t t t

38   Use with Lesson 31.

Distribute a pen and two pieces of typing paper to each student. Direct the students to warm up with their practice strokes and then to write three times each all of the letters written on the overhead. When several students have finished, ask for volunteers to show their papers. Direct attention to each paper and ask the class to comment on the letters, using the following terms.

1. Slant *(should be consistent and 13°)*
2. Pen angle *(should have serifs of 45° and thin diagonal strokes)*
3. Strokes *(should start and end in the correct place)*
4. Spacing within a word *(should have the most space between two straight strokes, less between a straight and a curved stroke, and the least between two curved strokes)*

Point out to the students that evaluating work in this fashion will help them learn to evaluate their own work.

Skill development

Demonstrate the formation of lowercase *s* and *t*—Write the letters on the lines on the overhead, verbalizing the direction of each stroke as you write.

Direct attention to the letter *s*—Point out the curve at the beginning of the stroke and that the top and bottom of the letter are reversed mirror images.

Swing up to the left,
Swerve around and
back to the left.

Direct attention to the letter *t*—Point out that the first stroke starts above the body line. The second stroke begins at the bottom of the body line and glides across to the right.

(1) Drop and curve right.
(2) Glide right.

Remind the students that the letters should not connect to the letters that follow.

Materials and Preparation

Have available:

- A chisel-point pen for each student.
- A guide sheet for each student.
- Two pieces of typing paper for each student.
- A transparency of the lowercase guide sheet.
- An overhead projector.
- An overhead pen.

——— Lesson Content ———

Introduction

Lead a critique session—On the overhead, write the following calligraphy letters, verbalizing the direction of each stroke as you write: *c, a, o, e, m, n, v, w, u, i,* and *r.*

See the calligraphy stroke descriptions in the Introduction.

Introduce spacing between words—Write the words *vow* and *crime* on the overhead. Lightly write an *o* between the words. Explain to the students that they should leave the space of an *o* between words.

Guided practice

Direct handwriting on worktext page 38—Review the calligraphy tip at the top of the page. Direct attention to the practice strokes. Point out that writing the practice strokes again will aid in better letter formation. Refer the students to the letter models on the lines at the bottom of the page. Remind them of the procedure for practicing the letters at the bottom of the page.

1. Note the arrow that indicates the direction of each stroke.
2. Trace the black letter with your finger.
3. Trace the gray letters with your pen.

Walk around the classroom to check that the students are making the correct strokes, both for practice strokes and for letter formation. Look for common errors.

Continued practice

Direct practice with typing paper and a guide sheet—Remind the students to use the side of the guide sheet labeled "Lowercase Guide Sheet." Tell each student to write the practice strokes, new letters, and the letters that were taught in the previous calligraphy lessons *(c, a, o, e, m, n, v, w, u, i,* and *r)*.

Write the word *sweater* on the overhead for the students to see. Point out that this word, along with the words *crime, ocean,* and *vow,* will provide good review and practice in word formation. Remind the students to leave the space of an *o* between words. Be sure to collect the pens when the students have finished.

sweater

People and Professions

Lighthouse Keeper and Botanist

The occupations presented in this unit, lighthouse keeper and botanist, may not be familiar to the students. The study of these occupations will broaden the students' general knowledge and provide them with some historical perspective while they review the letters *l* and *b*.

Read the whole unit, giving special attention to the calligraphy lesson at the end. Be sure to practice the calligraphy strokes ahead of time so that you will be well prepared to present the new letters.

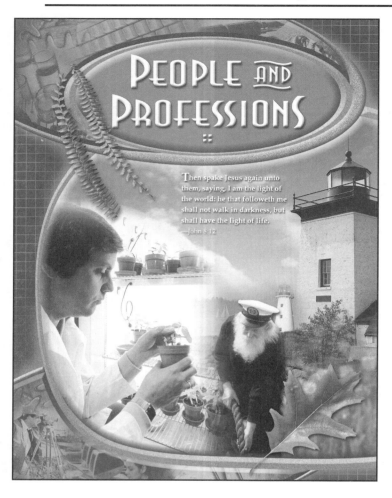

Abbie Burgess, Lighthouse Keeper

name_____

When Abbie Burgess was fourteen years old, her father was appointed the keeper of the two lighthouses on Matinicus Rock, a rock island twenty-two miles from the coast of Maine. Because the lighthouse lamps had to keep burning all night, Abbie tended the lighthouses whenever her father went to the coast for supplies. Although she was only fourteen years old, she managed to keep the lamps lit to protect the passing ships.

Write on handwriting paper the list of things Abbie had to do each morning to get the lamps ready to be lit at night.

1. Blow out the oil lamps in the tower.
2. Remove the glass chimneys after they cool.
3. Clean the oil lamp bowls.
4. Trim the wicks in the lamps.
5. Refill the lamps with oil.
6. Polish the silver reflectors in the tower.

40 Use with Lesson 32.

Materials and Preparation

Have available:
- Handwriting paper for each student.

Prepare:
- Handwriting lines on the chalkboard.

— Lesson Content —

Introduction

Introduce the unit—Direct the class to worktext page 39. Ask a student to read the unit verse. Ask how the function of a lighthouse relates to the statement that Jesus is the Light of the world. *(Lighthouses warn ships of danger and can help guide a ship to safety. Jesus, as the Light of the world, warns us of the dangers of sin and provides our salvation.)*

Direct attention to worktext page 40—Ask a student to read the story of Abbie Burgess at the top of the page.

Relate the following information.

For centuries, lighthouses have warned sailors of dangers that they could not see. Instead of using lanterns, the ancient Libyans filled metal baskets with burning wood and coal and hung them from poles at the top of high towers. Today's lighthouses send their signals from a huge lamp and lens that are sheltered in an enclosure of glass and steel. Some modern lighthouses also send radio signals; many are automatic. They do not require a keeper to take care of the equipment as they did when Abbie Burgess was growing up.

Skill development

Review the formation of *l*—Verbalize the direction of each stroke as you write the letters on the chalkboard. Point out that uppercase and lowercase *l* connect to letters that follow.

*Swing up,
Curve left and drop,
Loop left and sweep
across.*

**Swing up,
Curve left and loop.**

Demonstrate the writing of lowercase *l* in pairs—Point out that the pencil is not lifted between letters. Tell the students to air-trace the letters, and then allow volunteers to write the following words on the chalkboard.

hall   rebellion   dwell
hollow   small

Demonstrate alternate styles of writing the letter *l* (optional).

$\mathscr{L}$ $\mathscr{L}$ $\mathscr{L}$

Guided practice

Direct completion of worktext page 40—Allow a volunteer to read the list of things Abbie had to do each morning. Instruct the students to position their paper correctly before they begin writing.

Optional activity

Direct a writing activity—Direct each student to write the following list of types of illuminants that have been or are still used for lighthouse lamps.

wood fires   acetylene gas
coal   propane
oil lamp   electricity
vaporized oil burner

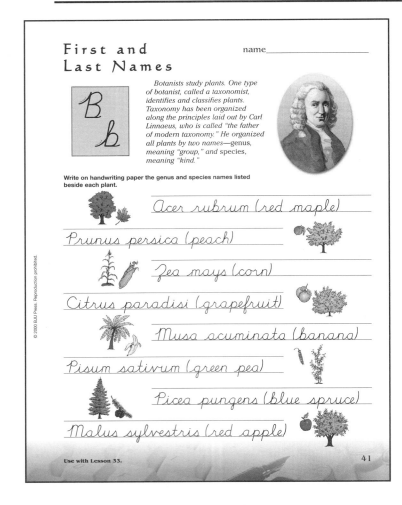

Skill development

Review the formation of *b*—Verbalize the direction of each stroke as you write the letters on the chalkboard. Point out that uppercase and lowercase *b* connect to the letters that follow.

Swing up and drop,
Retrace and swing around
  to lock,
Retrace and swing around
  to lock,
Sweep out.

Swing up,
Curve left and drop,
Retrace and swing around
  to lock,
Sweep out.

Demonstrate the writing of lowercase *b* in pairs—Point out that the pencil is not lifted between letters. Tell the class to air-trace the letters, and then allow volunteers to write the following words.

bubble   *stubborn*   *robber*   *scribble*

Demonstrate alternate styles of writing the letter *b* (optional).

Guided practice

Guide the completion of worktext page 42—Ask several students to read the scientific names of the plants pictured on this page. Check students' posture as they write the genus and species names of each plant on handwriting paper.

Optional activity

Direct a writing activity—On the chalkboard or on an overhead projector, write verses 1-6, 9-10, and 12 from the poem "Tapestry Trees" by William Morris. (See *Favorite Poems Old and New,* edited by Helen Ferris.) Do not include the names of the trees above the verses, but rather write them in a random order after you have written the verses. Direct each student to match the name of the tree to its description by writing the names of the trees on handwriting paper in the same order as the verses. When they are finished, go over the definitions of the following words.

Materials and Preparation

Have available:
- Handwriting paper for each student.

Prepare:
- Handwriting lines on the chalkboard.

— Lesson Content —

Introduction

Direct attention to worktext page 41—Ask a student to read the paragraph about botanists at the top of the page.

Relate further information about Linnaeus.

> Even though Carl Linnaeus began his professional training by going to medical school, he had been interested in plants ever since his boyhood in Sweden. He looked after a small botanical garden and began an insect collection. He also took several trips to study and collect plants. Later he became a professor of botany at the University of Uppsala and wrote books about plants and his special method of classifying them.

weal *(prosperity or happiness)*
bane *(fatal injury or ruin, a deadly poison)*
wain *(a large, open farm wagon)*
odorous *(fragrant)*

Also point out that the phrase "In my warm wave do fishes swim" could refer to the practice fishermen have of placing a drop of oil on the surface of troubled waters to calm them. The oil increases the surface tension of the water because it forms a film.

Lesson 34   Big and Bright   Worktext, page 42

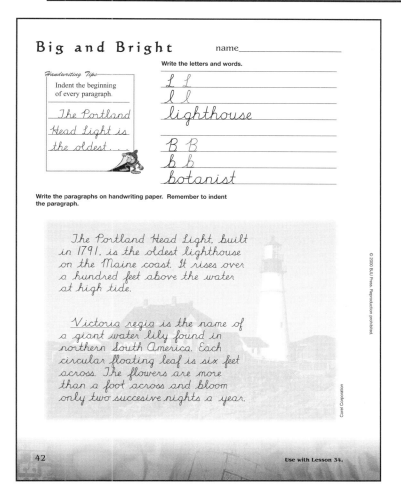

was named in honor of Queen Victoria, and in 1849 its first flower was presented to her.

Create interest in the lesson—Ask the students to pretend that they are botanists and have discovered a new plant that they will name after themselves. Give them a few minutes to think about their discovery, and then allow several students to describe their plant and tell its name.

Direct attention to worktext page 42—Explain that this page describes one of the oldest lighthouses and one of the largest lilies in the world.

Skill development

Focus on the handwriting tip on worktext page 42—Instruct the students that handwritten paragraphs should be indented approximately three spaces. Call attention to the handwriting tip at the top of the page.

Guided practice

Focus on writing the letters *l* and *b*—Point out the model letters at the top of worktext page 42. Remind the students that uppercase and lowercase *l* and *b* connect to letters that follow them. Tell the students to write the letters and words on the lines provided. Circulate among the students to check the formation of the letter *b*. Remind them that the uppercase and lowercase *b* lock on the base line and then sweep out.

Guide the completion of worktext page 42—Ask two students to read the paragraphs. Remind students to check posture, paper positioning, and pencil hold before beginning the handwriting activity. Also remind them to indent the two paragraphs.

Optional activity

Direct a writing activity—Direct each student to look up the following references about light in Scripture and list next to the reference the person, thing, or idea mentioned in the verse.

> I John 1:5 *(God)*
> Psalm 104:2 *(God)*
> John 1:4 *(Jesus)*
> Proverbs 6:23 *(the law)*
> Romans 13:12 *(armour)*
> Psalm 119:105 *(Word of God)*
> Matthew 5:14 *(Christians)*

Materials and Preparation

Have available:

- Handwriting paper for each student.

Lesson Content

Introduction

Relate the following information.

Your worktext page tells about a beautiful water lily, the *Victoria regia.* It was discovered more than one hundred years ago along the Amazon River in South America. This remarkable lily proved to be very difficult to grow, and its first seeds were sent to England in a bottle of water in order to keep them alive. The northern species of this water lily

Report: Old
Lighthouses of Maine

name_____

Steve's class had been learning about Maine in their Heritage Studies class. When his teacher told the class to choose a topic of interest about Maine and write a report about it, Steve immediately knew the topic of his report. He could not wait to find out more about the old lighthouses of Maine!

Self-evaluation	s	n
Posture		
Paper Positioning		
Pencil Hold		
Letter Formation		
Alignment		
Slant		
Spacing		
Neatness		

s=satisfactory   n=needs improvement

On handwriting paper, write the bibliography of the reference materials Steve used to write his report about lighthouses in Maine.

Bibliography

"A Strong Tower." *Portstown News*, January 12, 1996.

Blackmore, Thomas. *The First Lighthouse in America*.

Jackson, James. *Famous Lighthouse Keepers*.

"Lighthouses." *The National Encyclopedia*. 1997. XIII. 45–47.

"Maine." *The National Encyclopedia*. 1997. XIII. 192–221.

"The Keepers of the Maine Coast." *Oceans and Seas*. 1999.

Use with Lesson 35.   43

© 2000 BJU Press. Reproduction prohibited.

Materials and Preparation

Have available:

• Handwriting paper for each student.

Prepare:

• Handwriting lines on the chalkboard.
• The following sentence on the chalkboard.

  Mr. Lee Billings would like to build a new lighthouse on the Maine coast.

——— Lesson Content ———

Introduction

Lead a discussion—Tell the students to turn to worktext page 43. Ask a volunteer to read the paragraph at the top of the page. Remark that when Steve did the research for his report, he might have become curious about the men and women who used to take care of the old lighthouses. Ask what qualities a good lighthouse keeper should have. As suggestions are given, list them on the chalkboard. Mention that most often a lighthouse keeper was a man in his middle years who was also a fisherman. Besides doing odd jobs like carpentry, painting, masonry, and plastering, he had to be able to fix plumbing and broken machinery. A lighthouse was often tended by a man-and-wife team.

Skill development

Review the formation of *l* and *b*—Allow several students to write the letters on the chalkboard as you verbalize the stroke descriptions. Ask how these letters are alike. *(They both connect to letters that follow them.)* Point out how letters connect within the words in the sentence on the chalkboard. Direct a student to underline words containing the letter *l* or *b*. Allow several students to write the underlined words on the chalkboard, using your examples as models.

Assessment

Guide the completion of worktext page 43—Ask a student to read the instructions. Point out that the second line of the bibliography is indented approximately three spaces. Ask students to identify the punctuation marks used. Remind the students to underline the title of each book. Encourage them to use their best handwriting as they write the bibliography on handwriting paper.

You may want to use the evaluation form in the Appendix with this lesson. Be aware that the back of this page will be used in the next lesson on calligraphy.

Optional activity

Direct a writing activity—Draw attention to the fact that the primary function of a lighthouse is to produce light. Tell the students that without that light, lighthouses would not be able to warn ships of danger. Encourage each student to write a paragraph about lighthouses.

Distribute a pen and two pieces of typing paper to each student. Direct the students to warm up with their practice strokes and then to write three times each all of the letters written on the overhead. When the students have finished, ask for volunteers to show their papers. Direct attention to each paper and ask the class to comment on the letters, using the following terms.

1. Slant *(should be consistent and 13°)*
2. Pen angle *(should have serifs of 45° and thin diagonal strokes)*
3. Strokes *(should start and end in the correct place)*
4. Spacing within a word *(should have the most space between two straight strokes, less between a straight and a curved stroke, and the least between two curved strokes)*

Point out that evaluating work in this fashion will help them learn to evaluate their own work.

Review some of the terms relating to the guide sheet— Choose a student to demonstrate the terms relating to the guide sheet. *(the slant lines, the x-height, and these two guidelines: the base and body lines)* Ask another student to explain the reason for using the guide sheet. *(to control the height and slant of each stroke).*

Skill development

Demonstrate the formation of lowercase *x* and *z*—Write the letters on the lines on the overhead, verbalizing the direction of each stroke as you write. Show the students how the *x* is made up of two basic strokes.

Point out to the students that the letters should not connect to the letters that follow.

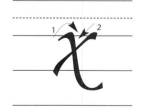

(1) Short diagonal right, Drop right below base line and curve.
(2) Drop left.

Short stroke up,
Glide right,
Drop left,
Swing right and curve up.

Materials and Preparation

Have available:

- A chisel-point pen for each student.
- A guide sheet for each student.
- Two pieces of typing paper for each student.
- A transparency of the lowercase guide sheet.
- An overhead projector.
- An overhead pen.

—— Lesson Content ——

Introduction

Lead a critique session—On the overhead or white board, write the following calligraphy letters, verbalizing the direction of each stroke as you write: *c, a, o, e, m, n, v, w, u, i,* and *r.*

See the calligraphy stroke descriptions in the Introduction.

Review spacing between words—Write the words *ocean* and *sweater* on the overhead. Lightly write an *o* between the words. Remind the students to leave the space of an *o* between words.

Guided practice

Direct handwriting on worktext page 44—Point out that writing the practice strokes will aid in better letter formation. Refer the students to the letter models on the lines at the bottom of the page. Remind them of the procedure for practicing the formation of the letters at the bottom of the page.

1. Note the arrow that indicates the direction of each stroke.
2. Trace the black letter with your finger.
3. Trace the gray letters with your pen.

Walk around the classroom to check that the students are making the correct strokes, both for practice strokes and for letter formation. Look for common errors.

Continued practice

Direct practice with typing paper and a guide sheet—Remind the students to use the side of the guide sheet labeled "Lowercase Guide Sheet." Tell each student to write the practice strokes, new letters, and the letters that were taught in the previous calligraphy lessons *(c, a, o, e, m, n, v, w, u, i, r, s,* and *t).*

Write the words *maze* and *six* on the overhead for the students to see. Point out that these words will provide good review and practice in word formation. Remind the students to leave the space of an *o* between words. Be sure to collect the pens when the students have finished.

People and Professions

Horticulturist and Kindergarten Teacher

This unit reviews the letters *h* and *k* and presents the occupations of the horticulturist and the kindergarten teacher. Once the students understand that the long name of the horticulturist (*hortus*—garden; *cultura*—culture) simply refers to a scientific gardener, they will find some personal applications for his expertise. They may be surprised at what can be learned about a kindergarten teacher.

In order to feel at ease with the calligraphy lesson at the end of this unit, you should begin now to practice the necessary strokes.

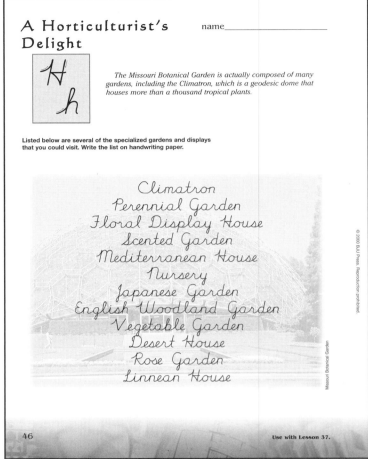

A Horticulturist's Delight

name_____

H h

The Missouri Botanical Garden is actually composed of many gardens, including the Climatron, which is a geodesic dome that houses more than a thousand tropical plants.

Listed below are several of the specialized gardens and displays that you could visit. Write the list on handwriting paper.

Climatron
Perennial Garden
Floral Display House
Scented Garden
Mediterranean House
Nursery
Japanese Garden
English Woodland Garden
Vegetable Garden
Desert House
Rose Garden
Linnean House

© 2000 BJU Press. Reproduction prohibited.

Missouri Botanical Garden

46   **Use with Lesson 37.**

Materials and Preparation

Have available:

- Handwriting paper for each student.

Prepare:

- Handwriting lines on the chalkboard.

—— Lesson Content ——

Introduction

Lead a discussion about the unit—Instruct the class to turn to worktext page 45. Discuss the unit page by asking questions such as the following.

1. What do you think a horticulturist does? *(He studies the best ways of growing plants like flowers, vegetables, and fruits.)*

2. What does a kindergarten teacher do? *(She teaches young children.)*

3. Who said the words of our unit verse? *(Jesus)*

4. What did Christ say we should do with His commandments? *(obey and teach them)*

5. What is the reward given to the person who obeys and teaches His commandments? *(He will be called great in the kingdom of heaven.)*

Introduce a famous garden.

The Missouri Botanical Garden, located in St. Louis, Missouri, was established by Henry Shaw in 1859. It has more than seventy-nine acres of flowering, fruit-bearing, and ornamental plants and trees. One of its most distinctive areas is the Scented Garden, which is filled with plants that are interesting to touch and smell. Alongside the plants are instructive Braille tablets for the blind to use. People from many countries visit the garden, not only to admire its beauty but also to learn about botany and horticulture from its library and its educational programs. It is considered to be one of the leading botanical gardens in the world.

Direct attention to worktext page 46—Ask a student to read the information at the top of the page.

Skill development

Review the formation of *h*—Verbalize the direction of each stroke as you write the letters on the chalkboard. Point out that lowercase *h* connects to letters that follow but that uppercase *h* does not.

(1) Swing up and drop.
(2) Drop and climb left,
*   Then glide right.*

Swing up,
Curve left and drop,
Retrace and swing right,
Drop and curve.

Demonstrate alternate styles of writing the letter *h* (optional).

Guided practice

Guide the completion of worktext page 46—Direct a student to read the instructions. Ask another student to read the list. As the students complete the page independently, check margins and letter formation.

Optional activity

Direct further thinking about plants—Direct each student to write a line or two about what attributes distinguish living things from nonliving things. Also tell him to write a sentence or two about why a further classification of living things separates plants from animals. *(Living things take in food, grow, move, and use oxygen and water. Plants are different from animals in that plants cannot move from place to place—although they do have internal movement—and in that they contain chlorophyll.)*

Kindergarten
Fun

name_____

Mrs. Fisher, an experienced kindergarten teacher, uses play dough to help her students learn important basic skills.

Play Dough

2 cups flour
4 tablespoons cream of tartar
1 cup salt
2 tablespoons oil
2 cups water
food coloring

Stir over low heat for approximately three minutes. When the mixture forms a ball, remove from heat. Store in airtight container. Do not refrigerate.

Write Mrs. Fisher's recipe for play dough on the lines below.

Use with Lesson 38.   47

Materials and Preparation

Prepare:

• Handwriting lines on the chalkboard.

——— Lesson Content ———

Introduction

Create interest in the lesson with the following information.

The word *kindergarten* comes from two German words that mean *child* and *garden*. Just as a garden is a special, protected spot for plants to grow, the kindergarten room can be an important place for the proper development of young children. With the help of a good teacher, students can develop a happy feeling about school and learn to get along with each other.

If you visit a kindergarten room and see the teacher hand out lumps of play dough to each student, you might think that the students are going to have play time. That is only partly correct. A kindergarten teacher often uses play dough to help the students learn the letters of the alphabet.

Sometimes the children form different letters with the play dough, or they roll out a play-dough pie and use a toothpick to write a certain alphabet letter on it.

Skill development

Review the formation of *k*—Verbalize the direction of each stroke as you write the letters on the chalkboard. Point out that both uppercase and lowercase *k* connect to letters that follow.

(1) Swing up and drop.
(2) Drop left,
    Then right and curve.

Swing up,
Curve left and drop,
Retrace and swing around
   to lock,
Drop right and curve.

Demonstrate the writing of lowercase *k* in pairs—Point out that the pencil is not lifted between letters. Allow several students to write the following words on the chalkboard.

knickknack   *bookkeeping*

Demonstrate alternate styles of writing the letter *k* (optional).

Guided practice

Guide the completion of worktext page 47—Tell the students to read the paragraph and the recipe. Direct them to complete the page independently.

Optional activity

Direct a writing activity—Explain to the students that as a teacher you are trying to foster an attitude of perseverance. (BAT: 2d Goal setting) Direct them to write the poem "Try, Try Again" by T. H. Palmer (*Favorite Poems Old and New,* edited by Helen Ferris).

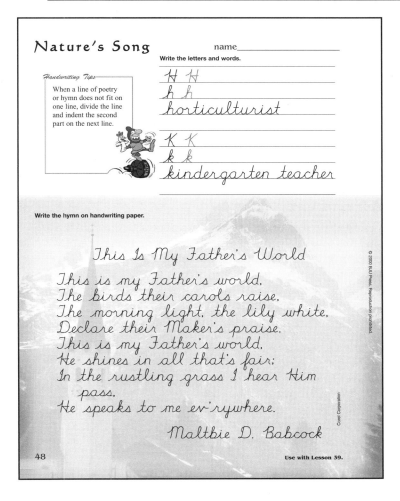

was very appreciative of nature. Early in the morning, he often would hike to his favorite hill to listen to the birds and talk to God. "I am going out to see my Father's world," he would tell the people in his church. "This Is My Father's World" has become a favorite hymn with many who love the outdoors.

Skill development

Focus on the handwriting tip on worktext page 48—Choose a student to read the handwriting tip at the top of the page. Refer the students to the line of poetry written on the chalkboard. Instruct a student to rewrite the line on the chalkboard, dividing the line and identifying the second part.

Guided practice

Focus on writing the letters *h* and *k*—Point out the model letters at the top of worktext page 48. Remind the students that lowercase *h* and uppercase and lowercase *k* connect to letters that follow. Instruct them to write the letters and words on the lines provided.

Guide the completion of worktext page 48—Ask a student to read the instructions. Direct the students to read the hymn silently and to complete the page independently.

Optional activity

Direct a writing activity—Direct each student to write out the words to another hymn about nature—"Fairest Lord Jesus."

Materials and Preparation

Have available:

- Handwriting paper for each student.

Prepare:

- Handwriting lines on the chalkboard.
- The following line of poetry on the chalkboard.

    This is my Father's world,

——— Lesson Content ———

Introduction

Relate the following background.

As a person who studies plants, a horticulturist can't help but be aware of God's beautiful creation. Maltbie Babcock, the man who wrote the hymn on our worktext page, was not a horticulturist, but he

Garden Strategy   name_____

Brian's uncle is a horticulturist. He helped Brian plan his vegetable garden so that it would produce more this year than it did last year. One thing that Brian learned was to keep tall crops from shading low-growing vegetables, making it possible for all plants to get plenty of sunlight.

On handwriting paper, draw a 4½" x 5" rectangle to represent Brian's garden. Write the names of vegetables on the plot in order of their height, beginning with the tallest plants.

Self-evaluation	s	n
Posture		
Paper Positioning		
Pencil Hold		
Letter Formation		
Alignment		
Slant		
Spacing		
Neatness		

s=satisfactory n=needs improvement

Royal Heritage beans 16"
Sweet Pickling cucumbers 8"
Dwarf Crinkled parsley 9"
Tenderheart beets 12"
Patio Gem tomatoes 3½'
Silver King corn 6'
Krockett's Giant peppers 3'
Midget Cherry radishes 6"
Harvey's Huge tomatoes 4'
Golden Wonder carrots 10"

Use with Lesson 40.   49

Materials and Preparation

Have available:

- Handwriting paper for each student.

Prepare:

- Handwriting lines on the chalkboard.

——— Lesson Content ———

Introduction

Provide the following information about plants.

> Our country is now able to produce better food in greater quantities because of what horticulturists have learned. These scientific gardeners have studied the characteristics of different soils and how plants grow best in them. They have also made discoveries that help in the fight against plant pests and diseases. All kinds of farmers and gardeners can do a better job by making use of the information available from horticulturists.

Direct attention to worktext page 49—Ask a student to read the paragraph about Brian's garden.

Skill development

Review the formation of *h* and *k*—Direct several students to write the letters on the chalkboard as you verbalize the stroke descriptions. Remind them that uppercase *h* does not connect with letters that follow. Allow volunteers to write the following words on the chalkboard.

Harvey   king   heart   Karl

Assessment

Guide the completion of worktext page 49—Instruct the students to read the directions and complete the page independently. Remind them to do the self-evaluation after they have finished the activity.

Answer key:

Silver King corn (6')
Harvey's Huge tomatoes (4')
Patio Gem tomatoes (3 ½')
Krockett's Giant peppers (3')
Royal Heritage beans (16")
Tenderheart beets (12")
Golden Wonder carrots (10")
Dwarf Crinkled parsley (9")
Sweet Pickling cucumbers (8")
Midget Cherry radishes (6")

You may want to use the evaluation form in the Appendix with this lesson. Be aware that the back of this page will be used in the next lesson on calligraphy.

Optional activity

Direct a writing activity— Tell the students that plant organs can be classified as either vegetative or reproductive. Explain that the vegetative organs are leaves, roots, and stems (roots and stems can be woody) and that the reproductive organs are flowers, fruits, and seeds. Direct each student to write down the terms *vegetative* and *reproductive,* listing the appropriate plant parts under them. Then ask each student to list as many food items as he can next to the items on the list. For example, *leaves—lettuce* and *roots—carrots.*

Calligraphy
Letters *b* and *d*

name_____

Calligraphy Tips

Plan your work on each line so that ascenders and descenders do not collide.

Copy the practice strokes.

Write the letters *b* and *d*.

50   Use with Lesson 41.

Materials and Preparation

Have available:

- A chisel-point pen for each student.
- A guide sheet for each student.
- Two pieces of typing paper for each student.
- A transparency of the lowercase guide sheet.
- An overhead projector.
- An overhead pen.

——— Lesson Content ———

Introduction

Lead a critique session—On the overhead, write the following calligraphy letters, verbalizing the direction of each stroke as you write: *c, a, o, e, m, n, v, w, u, i,* and *r.*

See the calligraphy stroke descriptions in the Introduction.

Distribute a pen and two pieces of typing paper to each student. Direct the students to warm up with their practice strokes and then to write three times each all of the letters written on the overhead. When the students have finished, ask for volunteers to show their papers. Direct attention to each paper and ask the class to comment on the letters, using the following terms.

1. Slant *(should be consistent and 13°)*
2. Pen angle *(should have serifs of 45° and thin diagonal strokes)*
3. Strokes *(should start and end in the correct place)*
4. Spacing within a word *(should have the most space between two straight strokes, less between a straight and a curved stroke, and the least between two curved strokes)*

Skill development

Demonstrate the formation of lowercase *b* and *d*—Write the letters on the lines on the overhead, verbalizing the direction of each stroke as you write. Point out to the students that the letters should not connect to the letters that follow. Point out that because both of the letters *b* and *d* have ascenders, the students will need to start close to the ascender line. Draw attention to the fact that the body of the *d* is the same basic form as the *c*. Inform the students that although the letters look quite the same, the *b* is a one-stroke letter and the *d* is a two-stroke letter. Tell them that the 13° letter slant will be a little more difficult because of the longer down stroke.

Glide left,
Drop,
Retrace and swing
around to lock.

(1) Glide left,
Swing around.
(2) Glide left,
Drop to lock and curve.

Guided practice

Direct handwriting on worktext page 50—Point out that writing the practice strokes will aid in better letter formation. Refer the students to the letter models on the lines at the bottom of the page. Remind them of the procedure for practicing the formation of the letters at the bottom of the page.

1. Note the arrow that indicates the direction of each stroke.
2. Trace the black letter with your finger.
3. Trace the gray letters with your pen.

Walk around the classroom to check that the students are making the correct strokes, both for practice strokes and for letter formation. Look for common errors. Be sure to collect the pens when the students have finished.

Continued practice

Direct practice with typing paper and a guide sheet—Remind the students to use the side of the guide sheet labeled "Lowercase Guide Sheet." Tell each student to write the practice strokes, new letters, and the letters that were taught in the previous calligraphy lessons *(c, a, o, e, m, n, v, w, u, i, r, s, t, x,* and *z).*

Write the word *board* on the overhead for the students to see. Point out that this word will provide good review and practice in word formation. Remind the students to leave the space of an *o* between words. Be sure to collect the pens when the students have finished.

Nurse and Meteorologist

The students are already familiar with the meteorologist (the weather forecaster) in a limited sense, and most of them have had experiences involving a nurse. In this unit they will be hearing about a famous nurse and learning of some weather instruments while they review the letters *m* and *n*.

Review and practice are important for developing your calligraphy skills too. Don't forget to look through this unit and prepare especially well for the calligraphy lesson.

A Noble Profession

name_____

In the 1800s, hospitals were only for the very poor who could not afford nurses in their homes. Since only untrained nurses worked in the hospitals, the patients did not receive proper care. Florence Nightingale trained at the Institution of Kaiserwerth in Germany to become a hospital nurse. She believed that nursing should be a noble profession, and she became devoted to the training of nurses and to the improvement of hospitals and public health.

Write on handwriting paper this list of positions held by today's graduate nurses.

General hospital duty
Private duty
Supervisory nursing
Administrative nursing
Industrial nursing
Nursing education
Public health nursing
Clinic nursing
Anesthetist
Surgical assistant
X-ray technician
Missionary nursing

Florence Nightingale
1820-1910

On the lines below write the quotations by Florence Nightingale.

"I shall succeed because I must."

"Nursing should be a noble profession."

52   Use with Lesson 42.

Materials and Preparation

Have available:

- Handwriting paper for each student.
- A dictionary.

Prepare:

- Handwriting lines on the chalkboard.

—— Lesson Content ——

Introduction

Introduce the unit—Tell the class to turn to worktext page 51. After a student tells which professions will be studied in this unit, instruct the class to read the verse in unison. Elicit from them the fact that a meteorologist studies the weather and reports on his observations. Ask the class what famous person they have often heard of in connection with the nursing profession. *(Florence Nightingale)*

Introduce Florence Nightingale.

Florence Nightingale grew up in a wealthy family and lived in a beautiful home, but even as a little girl she was concerned about the poor and the sick. One day she decided that she wanted to become a nurse. Her family was so upset that it took her five years to persuade them to let her start training. After graduation she began working to improve the dirty, poorly managed hospitals of her country so that sick people could get better treatment. During the Crimean War, she volunteered to go and help care for the thousands of wounded British soldiers. In the army hospital she found patients lying neglected on the floor while rats scampered through the filthy rooms. The doctors did not welcome her because they thought that she and the other nurses would interfere with their work. Florence's calm efficiency changed their minds, and before long the nurses were allowed to clean up the wards and take care of the soldiers.

Direct attention to worktext page 52—Ask a student to read the information at the top of the page and the two quotations at the bottom of the page. Ask what the word *noble* means. If necessary, ask a student to look it up in the dictionary. *(noble—having or showing qualities of high character, as courage or generosity)* Explain to the class that before Florence did her work to improve the nursing profession, nurses in public hospitals were often untrained and careless. Because of her example and influence, people collected money for a Nightingale Fund, and Florence used it to start a training school for nurses.

Skill development

Review the formation of *n*—Verbalize the direction of each stroke as you write the letters on the chalkboard. Point out that uppercase and lowercase *n* connect to letters that follow.

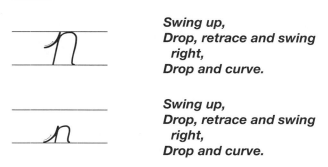

Swing up,
Drop, retrace and swing
*   right,*
Drop and curve.

Swing up,
Drop, retrace and swing
*   right,*
Drop and curve.

Demonstrate the writing of lowercase *n* in pairs—Write the words *connect* and *channel* on the chalkboard. Allow several students to write them, using your examples as models.

Demonstrate alternate styles of writing the letter *n* (optional).

Guided practice

Guide the completion of worktext page 52—Ask a student to read the two sets of directions. Check letter formation as the students complete the two activities.

Optional activity

Direct a poetry activity—Remind the students that Florence Nightingale nursed many soldiers during the Crimean War. Tell them that hundreds of men were killed when the Light Brigade made a heroic but extremely dangerous charge in obedience to the orders of an unwise commander. Instruct each student to use handwriting paper to write the first stanza of the poem "The Charge of the Light Brigade" (*Favorite Poems Old and New,* edited by Helen Ferris). Interested students may read the rest of the poem for themselves.

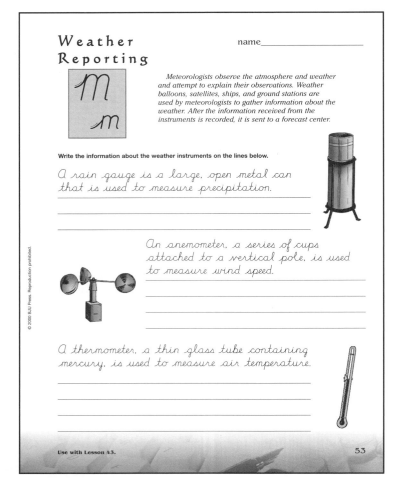

Direct attention to worktext page 53—Ask a student to read the information about meteorologists at the top of the page.

Skill development

Review the formation of *m*—Verbalize the direction of each stroke as you write the letters on the chalkboard. Point out that uppercase and lowercase *m* connect to letters that follow.

Swing up,
Drop, retrace and swing
  right,
Drop, retrace and swing
  right,
Drop and curve.

Swing up,
Drop, retrace and swing
  right,
Drop, retrace and swing
  right,
Drop and curve.

Demonstrate the writing of lowercase *m* in pairs—Point out that the pencil is not lifted between letters. Tell the class to air-trace the letters. Write the words *mammoth* and *summit* on the chalkboard. Allow volunteers to write them, using your examples as models.

Demonstrate alternate styles of writing the letter *m* (optional).

Guided practice

Guide the completion of worktext page 53—Direct a student to read the instructions. Choose volunteers to read the three sentences about weather instruments. Encourage the students to write the sentences neatly as they complete the page.

Optional activity

Direct a writing activity—Instruct each student to use handwriting paper to write a paragraph describing the kind of weather he dislikes the most and why. Remind him to use lively verbs.

Materials and Preparation

Have available:

- A Bible for each student.

Prepare:

- Handwriting lines on the chalkboard.

——— Lesson Content ———

Introduction

Direct a choral reading—Tell the class to turn to Psalm 147, which contains the unit verse. Comment that the psalmist sounds as if he could have been an amateur meteorologist. Divide the class into two groups and instruct them to read the entire psalm as follows: verses 1-2, all together; verses 3-18, responsively; verses 19-20, all together. Ask a volunteer to re-read verse 11. Point out that of all the beautiful things the Lord has made, an obedient heart delights Him the most. (BAT 2b: Servanthood)

The Wind and the Sun

name_____

Write the letters and words.

Handwriting Tips

Quotation marks set off the exact words a person speaks.

"I'm stronger," said the Wind.

n n
n n
nurse
m m
m m
meteorologist

Write the fable on handwriting paper. Include the quotation marks.

> One day the Wind and the Sun were arguing about which was stronger. The Wind boasted, "I'm stronger because I can wave a flag, whistle a tune, and sail a ship!"
>
> Soon a traveler came walking down the road. The Sun challenged the Wind, "Whichever of us can force the traveler to take off his coat will be the stronger one. You may try first."
>
> Then the Sun hid behind a cloud, and the Wind began to blow. But the harder he blew, the tighter the traveler wrapped his coat around him.
>
> Finally the Sun shouted, "Stop!"
>
> It was the Sun's opportunity to shine now. And he shone so brightly that the traveler became too hot and had to remove his coat before he could finish his journey.
>
> Moral: Kindness has a greater effect than sternness.

54   Use with Lesson 44.

Materials and Preparation

Have available:

- Handwriting paper for each student.

Prepare:

- The following sentence on the chalkboard.

   I can wave a flag, said the Wind.

——— Lesson Content ———

Introduction

Introduce Aesop.

The story on today's worktext page is called a fable. (Review the meaning of *fable:* a special kind of short story that usually has animal characters. It teaches a lesson, called a "moral.") The fable we will read today is one of many told by Aesop, a skillful storyteller who was a Greek slave. Not very many facts are known about Aesop because he lived in the sixth century B.C. There is a legend that he saved the king of Athens from being mobbed by a crowd of his angry subjects. According to the legend, Aesop appeased the crowd by telling them a fable about a group of frogs who decided one day that they wanted a king. The frogs ended up with a stork for a king, and they were very upset when the stork began eating them. The moral of the story was "Let well enough alone." Although Aesop began life as a slave, his master was so impressed by his witty fables that he made him a free man.

Skill development

Focus on the handwriting tip on worktext page 54— Read aloud the handwriting tip and the sentence in the box at the top of the page. Remind the students that the quotation marks are written before and after the exact words spoken. Direct attention to the sentence on the chalkboard. Ask a student to tell where the quotation marks belong in the sentence. Write the quotation marks in the sentence.

Guided practice

Focus on writing the letters *n* and *m*—Remind the students that uppercase and lowercase letters *n* and *m* connect to the letters that follow them. Direct attention to the top of worktext page 54. Instruct the students to practice the letters and words on the lines provided.

Direct the completion of worktext page 54—Ask a student to read the fable aloud. Then direct the students to write the fable on handwriting paper. Remind them to write quotation marks to set off the exact words spoken by the Wind and the Sun.

Optional activity

Direct a word study—Ask each student to use handwriting paper to write synonyms for the following words from the fable on worktext page 54.

stronger	*force*	*wrapped*
first	*hid behind*	*brightly*
shouted	*harder*	*remove*
walk	*tighten*	*finish*

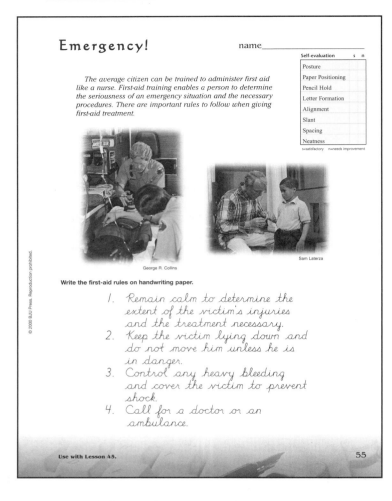

Emergency!   name_____

Self-evaluation	s	n
Posture		
Paper Positioning		
Pencil Hold		
Letter Formation		
Alignment		
Slant		
Spacing		
Neatness		

The average citizen can be trained to administer first aid like a nurse. First-aid training enables a person to determine the seriousness of an emergency situation and the necessary procedures. There are important rules to follow when giving first-aid treatment.

s=satisfactory   n=needs improvement

George R. Collins   Sam Laterza

Write the first-aid rules on handwriting paper.

1. Remain calm to determine the extent of the victim's injuries and the treatment necessary.
2. Keep the victim lying down and do not move him unless he is in danger.
3. Control any heavy bleeding and cover the victim to prevent shock.
4. Call for a doctor or an ambulance.

Use with Lesson 45.   55

1. He was not a nurse.
2. He was not a Jew.
3. He is not in the Old Testament.
4. Jesus told a story about him.
5. He is remembered because he showed mercy.
6. Thieves are part of the story.
7. The injured man was ignored by other travelers.
8. The story is found in Luke 10.

After the class has guessed who the man is, elicit from them a brief outline of the story. If necessary, they may turn in their Bibles to the account in Luke 10:30-37.

Direct attention to worktext page 55—Ask a volunteer to read the paragraph at the top of the page.

Skill development

Review the formation of *n* and *m*—Allow several students to write the letters on the chalkboard as you verbalize the stroke descriptions. Remind the students that these letters connect to letters that follow them. Allow volunteers to write the following sentences on the chalkboard.

> *Remain calm during an emergency.*
>
> *Do not move the injured victim.*

Assessment

Guide the completion of worktext page 55—Ask volunteers to read the four first-aid rules. Direct the students to complete the page independently Remind them to do the self-evaluation after they have finished the activity.

You may want to use the evaluation form in the Appendix with this lesson. Be aware that the back of this page will be used in the next lesson on calligraphy.

Materials and Preparation

Have available:

- Handwriting paper for each student.
- A Bible for each student.

Prepare:

- Handwriting lines on the chalkboard.

——— Lesson Content ———

Introduction

Create interest in today's lesson—Explain that today's lesson is about first aid. Tell the students that you are thinking of a Bible character who administered first aid. Give them the following clues until they guess the character. *(the Good Samaritan)*

Optional activity

Direct a reasoning activity—Ask each student to re-read the first-aid rules on worktext page 55 and to think of an answer to the question "why?" for each rule. Instruct him to write his answer on handwriting paper.

Materials and Preparation

Have available:

- A chisel-point pen for each student.
- A guide sheet for each student.
- Two pieces of typing paper for each student.
- A transparency of the lowercase guide sheet.
- An overhead projector.
- An overhead pen.

——— Lesson Content ———

Introduction

Review the calligraphy terms—Direct the students to answer the following questions.

1. What are the names of the two guidelines on the lowercase guide sheet? *(body line and base line)*
2. What is x-height? *(the distance between the base and body lines; equal to five pen widths)*
3. What is a stroke? *(a single mark formed with a pen)*
4. What should the pen angle be? *(45 °)*
5. What is the proper slant of the letters? *(13 °)*

Skill development

Demonstrate the formation of lowercase *f* and *l*—Write the letters on the lines on the overhead, verbalizing the direction of each stroke as you write. Ask the students if they see a similarity between the *l* and any previous letters. *(It is the same as the second stroke of the* d.*)* Direct attention to the fact that the *l* starts just below the ascender lines. Ask the students to name the new feature of the *f.* *(a descender line)* Direct attention to the fact that *f* starts almost at the ascender line and goes almost to the descender line. Point out that this is one of the more difficult letters because of the long, continuous stroke. Help the students to understand that their hands and arms will have to move slightly downward in order to form this letter smoothly and keep a consistent letter slant. Point out that the letters should not connect to the letters that follow.

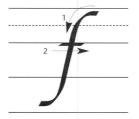

**(1) Glide left,
    Drop low and hook left.
(2) Cross right below the
    body line.**

**Glide left,
Drop and curve.**

Guided practice

Direct handwriting on worktext page 56—Refer the students to the letter models on the lines at the bottom of the page. Remind them of the procedure for practicing the formation of the letters at the bottom of the page.

1. Note the arrow that indicates the direction of each stroke.
2. Trace the black letter with your finger.
3. Trace the gray letters with your pen.

Walk around the classroom to check that the students are making the correct strokes, both for practice strokes and for letter formation. Look for common errors.

Continued practice

Direct practice with typing paper and a guide sheet—Remind the students to use the side of the guide sheet labeled "Lowercase Guide Sheet." Tell each student to write the practice strokes, new letters, and the letters that were taught in the previous calligraphy lessons *(c, a, o, e, m, n, v, w, u, i, r, s, t, x, z, d,* and *b)*.

Write the word *flawless* on the overhead for the students to see. Tell them that this word will provide good review and practice in word formation. Remind the students to leave the space of an *o* between words. Be sure to collect the pens when the students have finished.

flawless

PEOPLE AND PROFESSIONS

Pilot and Radiobroadcaster

Most sixth-graders think that piloting an airplane or broadcasting over the radio is an exciting job. In this unit they will have a chance to learn about some of the technical aspects of these occupations. The letters presented for review are *p* and *r*.

You will want to read the entire unit at this time, noting the new letters that are to be introduced in the calligraphy lesson. Remember to practice forming the letters before you present them to your students.

And he said unto them, Go ye into all the world, and preach the gospel to every creature.
—Mark 16:15

Ready for Takeoff   name_____

Pilots of commercial airplanes are fully responsible for passengers, cargo, and mail carried on the plane. The flight engineer, pilot, and copilot work as a team to check the instruments and the condition of the craft before takeoff. Even though commercial airplanes are not military vehicles, they are kept "shipshape" under the authority of the pilot, who is officially in command of his flight.

Write the three paragraphs about the kinds of airplane instruments.

Flight instruments indicate an airplane's speed, its position in relation to the earth's surface, and its planned flight path.

Engine instruments monitor the performance of the engines on the airplane. They indicate the engine's temperature and fuel consumption.

Aircraft systems' instruments are needed to check the electrical, hydraulic, fuel, and air-conditioning systems of the airplane.

www.arttoday.com

© 2000 BJU Press. Reproduction prohibited.

58   Use with Lesson 47.

Materials and Preparation

Have available:
- Handwriting paper for each student.

Prepare:
- Handwriting lines on the chalkboard.

—— Lesson Content ——

Introduction

Lead a discussion—Tell the students to turn to worktext page 57 and read the unit verse silently. Ask how the pilot and the radiobroadcaster make it possible for modern missionaries to obey this command. *(The pilot can transport missionaries and supplies to the most inaccessible areas of the world. He also provides emergency medical transportation, which gives missionaries moral and physical support. Radiobroadcasters can send their gospel programs over natural obstacles such as bodies of water and also can reach people who do not have religious freedom. By means of radio, the gospel can be preached to people in distant places and in many languages.)*

Direct attention to worktext page 58—Ask a student to read the paragraph about commercial pilots.

Skill development

Review the formation of *p*—Verbalize the direction of each stroke as you write the letters on the chalkboard. Point out that uppercase *p* does not connect to the letters following it but that lowercase *p* does. Tell the students to note the connecting of the letter *p* to letters that follow.

***Swing up and drop,
Retrace and swing around
   to lock.***

***Swing up,
Drop low,
Retrace and swing around
   to lock,
Sweep out.***

Demonstrate the writing of lowercase *p* in pairs—Write *p* in pairs on the chalkboard as the students air-trace the letters. Choose several students to come to the chalkboard to write the following words containing a double *p*.

ripple   *stopper*   *apple*

Demonstrate alternate styles of writing the letter *p* (optional).

Guided practice

Guide completion of worktext page 58—Allow volunteers to read the paragraphs about airplane instruments. Direct the students to write the paragraphs on handwriting paper.

Optional activity

Direct a writing activity—Explain to the class that Orville and Wilbur Wright, pioneers in building airplanes, applied for a patent in 1903 to protect their invention. Tell each student to look up and copy from a dictionary the meaning of *patent*. Then ask him to write on handwriting paper the following explanation that the Wright brothers included in their letter.

> The relative movements of the air and aeroplane may be derived from the motion of the air in the form of wind blowing in the direction opposite to that in which the apparatus is traveling or by a combined downward and forward movement of the machine, as in starting from an elevated position or by combination of these two things.

Lesson 48   Sound Waves to Radio Waves   Worktext, page 59

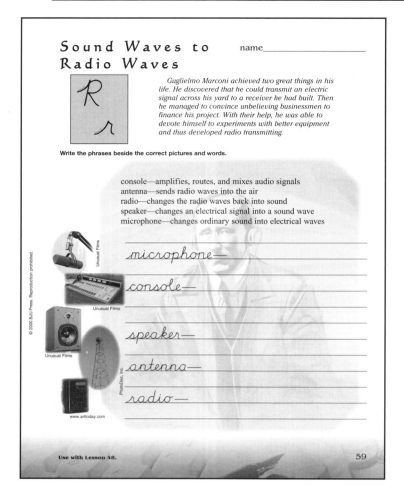

Sound Waves to
Radio Waves

name_____

Guglielmo Marconi achieved two great things in his life. He discovered that he could transmit an electric signal across his yard to a receiver he had built. Then he managed to convince unbelieving businessmen to finance his project. With their help, he was able to devote himself to experiments with better equipment and thus developed radio transmitting.

Write the phrases beside the correct pictures and words.

console—amplifies, routes, and mixes audio signals
antenna—sends radio waves into the air
radio—changes the radio waves back into sound
speaker—changes an electrical signal into a sound wave
microphone—changes ordinary sound into electrical waves

microphone—

console—

speaker—

antenna—

radio—

Use with Lesson 48.   59

Materials and Preparation

Prepare:

- Handwriting lines on the chalkboard.
- The following sentence on the chalkboard.

  A radio transmitter produces radio waves.

———— Lesson Content ————

Introduction

Introduce Marconi.

Guglielmo Marconi (1874-1937) was an Italian inventor and electrical engineer. When he was growing up, he read many books from the large scientific library in his home. He became interested in electromagnetic waves and later experimented with equipment that could send and receive radio waves over long distances. Since the Italian government was not interested in his ideas, he went to England to find some way of getting money so that he could begin a wireless telegraph company. Our worktext page tells what happened next.

Direct attention to worktext page 59—Ask a student to read the paragraph about Marconi.

Skill development

Review the formation of *r*—Verbalize the direction of each stroke as you write the letters on the chalkboard. Point out that both uppercase and lowercase *r* connect to letters that follow. Direct attention to the sentence on the chalkboard.

***Swing up and drop,
Retrace and swing around
 to lock,
Drop right and curve.***

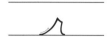

***Swing up,
Slide right,
Drop and curve.***

Demonstrate the writing of lowercase *r* in pairs—Write *r* in pairs on the chalkboard as the students air-trace the letters. Allow several students to write the following words on the chalkboard.

hurry   *tomorrow*   *current*

Demonstrate alternate styles of writing the letter *r* (optional).

Guided practice

Guide the completion of worktext page 60—Explain that the terms listed are components used in radio broadcasting. Allow volunteers to read the words and phrases. Encourage the students to write the phrases neatly as they complete the page independently.

Optional activity

Direct a testimony activity—Tell each student to imagine that he has been invited to give his testimony on a radio broadcast to a Communist country. Ask him to write out his story on handwriting paper. He should include his favorite Bible verse and a few sentences about his relationship with the Lord, or when and how he was saved.

The Spirit of St. Louis

name_____

Handwriting Tips

The consistency of the slant of letters is important for legible writing.

pilot
pilot

Write the letters and words, using a consistent slant.

P P
p p
pilot
R R
r r
radiobroadcaster

Charles Lindbergh was only twenty-five years old when he made the first solo flight across the Atlantic Ocean in 1927. He flew from Roosevelt Field near New York City to Le Bourget Field near Paris, France, in his single-engine airplane The Spirit of St. Louis. *Lindbergh completed the 3,600-mile flight in 33 ½ hours.*

Before Lindbergh flew from New York City, he had flown his plane from San Diego, California, to St. Louis, Missouri, and then to New York City. After the historic trans-Atlantic flight, he visited several European cities and three American cities, where he was greeted with celebrations and parades.

On handwriting paper write the names of cities that Lindbergh visited.

San Diego, California
St. Louis, Missouri
New York City
Paris, France

Brussels, Belgium
London, England
Washington, D.C.

60   **Use with Lesson 49.**

Materials and Preparation

Have available:

- Handwriting paper for each student.

Prepare:

- Handwriting lines on the chalkboard.
- The following words on the chalkboard.

  airspeed

  indicator

  altimeter

  turn-and-bank indicator

  horizon indicator

  rate-of-climb indicator

- The following words on the handwriting lines using inconsistent slant.

  pilot   *radiobroadcaster*

——— Lesson Content ———

Introduction

Direct a game—Appoint a student to be "captain" of a plane. As you read each of the following sentences, the captain may choose a student to match the definition with the flight instruments listed on the chalkboard. Each student who answers correctly may stand beside the captain and become part of his "crew."

1. It shows the plane's position in relation to the earth's surface. *(horizon indicator)*
2. It shows how fast the airplane is flying. *(airspeed indicator)*
3. It shows how fast the airplane is climbing or descending. *(rate-of-climb indicator)*
4. It helps the pilot know how far he is above the ground. *(altimeter)*
5. It shows the pilot whether he is making a turn correctly. *(turn-and-bank indicator)*

Direct attention to worktext page 60—Ask a student to read the story of Charles Lindbergh's flight. Point out that this early aviator did not have the benefit of the complicated instruments that pilots use today.

Skill development

Focus on the handwriting tip on worktext page 60—Read aloud the handwriting tip in the box at the top of the page. Remind the students that the slant of the letters should be consistent. Direct attention to the words on the chalkboard. Point out the inconsistent slant. Then call on two students to write the words using a consistent slant.

Guided practice

Focus on writing the letters *p* and *r*—Refer the students to the model letters at the top of worktext page 60. Remind them that uppercase *r* and lowercase *p* and *r* connect to letters that follow them. Instruct the students to practice the letters and words on the lines provided.

Direct the completion of worktext page 60—Ask a student to read the directions and the cities listed. Remind the students to use a consistent slant as they write the names of the cities on handwriting paper.

Optional activity

Assign a world trip—Ask each student to make a list of the cities or countries he would like to visit on an airplane flight around the world. Remind him to capitalize correctly.

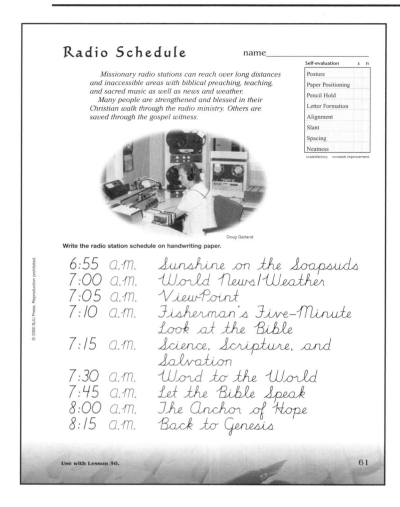

Radio Schedule   name_____

Missionary radio stations can reach over long distances and inaccessible areas with biblical preaching, teaching, and sacred music as well as news and weather.
Many people are strengthened and blessed in their Christian walk through the radio ministry. Others are saved through the gospel witness.

Self-evaluation	s	n
Posture		
Paper Positioning		
Pencil Hold		
Letter Formation		
Alignment		
Slant		
Spacing		
Neatness		

s=satisfactory n=needs improvement

Doug Garland

Write the radio station schedule on handwriting paper.

6:55 a.m.   Sunshine on the Soapsuds
7:00 a.m.   World News/Weather
7:05 a.m.   ViewPoint
7:10 a.m.   Fisherman's Five-Minute
             Look at the Bible
7:15 a.m.   Science, Scripture, and
             Salvation
7:30 a.m.   Word to the World
7:45 a.m.   Let the Bible Speak
8:00 a.m.   The Anchor of Hope
8:15 a.m.   Back to Genesis

Use with Lesson 50.   61

© 2000 BJU Press. Reproduction prohibited.

Materials and Preparation

Have available:

- Handwriting paper for each student.

Prepare:

- Handwriting lines on the chalkboard.

—— Lesson Content ——

Introduction

Play a review game—Choose students to tell the occupation that matches each person listed below.

1. Carl Linnaeus *(botanist)*
2. Thomas Edison *(inventor)*
3. Charles Lindbergh *(pilot)*

4. Abbie Burgess *(lighthouse keeper)*
5. Simon Peter *(fisherman)*
6. Florence Nightingale *(nurse)*

Direct attention to worktext page 61—Ask a student to read the paragraphs about Christian radio broadcasting.

Skill development

Review the formation of *p* and *r*—Allow several students to write the letters on the chalkboard as you verbalize the stroke descriptions. Remind them that lowercase *r* and *p* connect to the letters that follow them but that uppercase *p* does not. Choose volunteers to write the following words on the chalkboard.

Pastor   prayer   Radio   reading

Assessment

Guide the completion of worktext page 62—Ask a student to read the radio schedule aloud. Explain that the picture and the schedule are from a missionary radio station in the Caribbean. Encourage the students to do their best as they write the time schedule on handwriting paper.

You may want to use the evaluation form in the Appendix with this lesson. Be aware that the back of this page will be used in the next lesson on calligraphy.

Optional activity

Direct a schedule-writing activity—Tell each student to use handwriting paper to make a schedule of what they usually do on Saturdays. It may be real or imaginary. Ask him to include the beginning time of each activity, using the format on worktext page 61.

Calligraphy Letters *h* and *k*

---- **Lesson Content** ----

Introduction

Direct a warm-up activity—Direct the students to write three of each of their practice strokes on typing paper. Then direct them to write as many words as they can think of from the letters that they have had so far *(c, a, o, e, m, n, v, w, u, i, r, s, t, x, z, d, b, f,* and *l)*.

Skill development

Demonstrate the formation of lowercase *h* and *k*—Write the letters on the lines on the overhead, verbalizing the direction of each stroke as you write. Point out the similarities between the start of the letter *b* and the letters *h* and *k*. Make special note of how the stroke is the same through the retrace and the swing. Inform the students that as with the *b,* the *h* is a one-stroke letter. Also point out that both of these letters start close to the ascender line. Point out that the letters should not connect to the letters that follow.

Glide left,
Drop,
Retrace and swing right,
Drop and curve.

(1) Glide left,
    Drop.
(2) Glide left and drop left
    halfway between
    body and base lines.
(3) Drop right below base
    line and curve.

Materials and Preparation

Have available:

- A chisel-point pen for each student.
- A guide sheet for each student.
- Two pieces of typing paper for each student.
- A transparency of the lowercase guide sheet.
- An overhead projector.
- An overhead pen.

Guided practice

Direct handwriting on worktext page 62—Refer the students to the letter models on the lines at the bottom of the page. Remind them of the procedure for practicing the formation of the letters at the bottom of the page.

1. Note the arrow that indicates the direction of each stroke.
2. Trace the black letter with your finger.
3. Trace the gray letters with your pen.

Walk around the classroom to check that the students are making the correct strokes, both for practice strokes and for letter formation. Look for common errors.

Continued practice

Have the students continue to practice with typing paper and a guide sheet—Tell the students to design a pattern of three rows containing a pair of letters repeated five times per row (see example). They should choose two of the letters they have learned *(c, a, o, e, m, n, v, w, u, i, r, s, t, x, z, d, b, f,* and *l).* When they have completed the pattern, have them look at the alignment of the letters to see the consistency of the slant. Explain that they should avoid "rivers of white" running down the page.

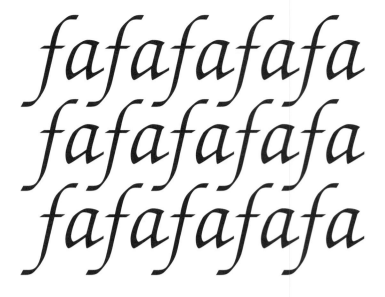

Veterinarian and Xylographer

The letters to be practiced in this unit are *v* and *x*. Most children are curious about animals, and we have chosen the veterinarian to represent the letter *v*. The art of the xylographer, or wood carver, is fast becoming obsolete in our modern world, but the students will enjoy exploring an unusual occupation as well as having the fun of learning a new, rather peculiar word.

Please read the entire unit, paying particular attention to the last lesson on calligraphy. You will find it helpful at this time to begin practicing the strokes for the new calligraphy letters.

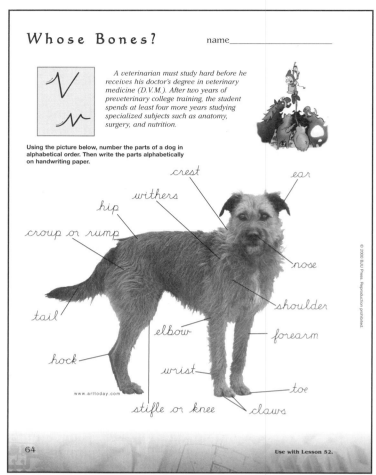

Materials and Preparation

Have available:

- Handwriting paper for each student.

Prepare:

- Handwriting lines on the chalkboard.

——— Lesson Content ———

Introduction

Introduce the unit—Tell the class to turn to worktext page 63. Ask a student to read the unit verse. Explain that this unit is about veterinarians and xylographers. Tell the students that a xylographer is an artist who does woodcarvings and wood cuts. Allow class members to tell of experiences they have had involving their pets and a veterinarian.

Relate the following information.

Many people have reason to be glad that we have well-trained veterinarians in our country. The veterinarian who works in a large city can treat sick pets in pet hospitals that have life-saving equipment similar to that of regular hospitals. An important kind of veterinarian is one who takes care of farm animals, because some animal diseases can be passed on to human beings. The farmer is happy to have a veterinarian inoculate his animals against certain diseases because he can lose a lot of money if his whole herd of cows or pigs gets sick and dies. Circuses and zoos also depend on veterinarians to keep their animals healthy.

Direct attention to worktext page 64—Ask a student to read the paragraph about veterinary students. Explain that in the study of anatomy, students learn about the structure of the animals they will be treating. For example, they must memorize the names of a dog's bones and the different parts of its body.

Skill development

Review the formation of *v*—Verbalize the direction of each stroke as you write the letters on the chalkboard. Point out that uppercase *v* does not connect to letters that follow but that lowercase *v* does.

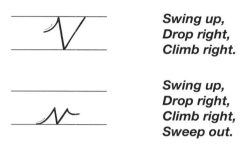

Swing up,
Drop right,
Climb right.

Swing up,
Drop right,
Climb right,
Sweep out.

Demonstrate the writing of the letter *v*—Write the following words on the chalkboard.

veterinarian   *vaccinate*

Allow several students to write the words, using your examples as models.

Demonstrate alternate styles of writing the letter *v* (optional).

Guided practice

Guide the completion of worktext page 64—Ask a student to read the directions. Ask another student to read the names of the parts of a dog's body. Direct the students to complete the activity independently.

Optional activity

Direct a writing activity—Instruct each student to list on handwriting paper the bones of a dog that have the same names as those in the human body. (This information is available in a dictionary.)

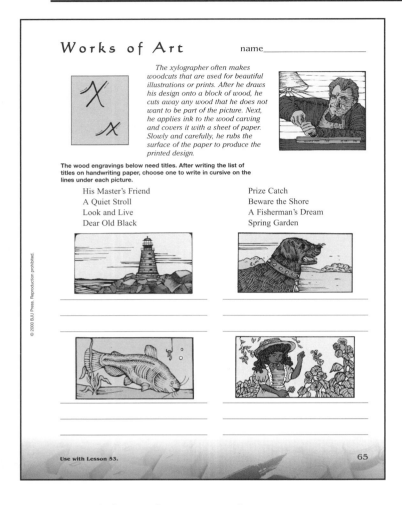

Works of Art   name_____

The xylographer often makes woodcuts that are used for beautiful illustrations or prints. After he draws his design onto a block of wood, he cuts away any wood that he does not want to be part of the picture. Next, he applies ink to the wood carving and covers it with a sheet of paper. Slowly and carefully, he rubs the surface of the paper to produce the printed design.

The wood engravings below need titles. After writing the list of titles on handwriting paper, choose one to write in cursive on the lines under each picture.

His Master's Friend
A Quiet Stroll
Look and Live
Dear Old Black

Prize Catch
Beware the Shore
A Fisherman's Dream
Spring Garden

Use with Lesson 53.   65

© 2000 BJU Press. Reproduction prohibited.

have undergone many changes in the past century but are still used for book illustrations and enjoyed as fine works of art.

Direct attention to worktext page 65—Ask a student to read the information at the top of the page.

Skill development

Review the formation of *x*—Verbalize the direction of each stroke as you write the letters on the chalkboard. Point out that uppercase and lowercase *x* are crossed after the entire word is written. Remind the students that uppercase and lowercase *x* connect to letters that follow them.

(1) Swing up,
Drop right and curve.
(2) Drop left.

(1) Swing up,
Drop right and curve.
(2) Drop left.

Demonstrate the writing of the letter *x*—Write the following words on the chalkboard.

xylographer   *excellent*

Allow several students to write the words, using your examples as models.

Demonstrate alternate styles of writing the letter *x* (optional).

Guided practice

Guide the completion of worktext page 65—Direct a student to read the instructions. Remind the students to capitalize the titles as they write them on handwriting paper and then as they write one below each picture. Instruct them to complete the page independently.

Optional activity

Direct a deciphering activity—Write the following ciphers on the chalkboard. Explain that ciphers are simply sentences with the spaces rearranged. Ask the students to decipher the sentences and then to write them on handwriting paper.

Materials and Preparation

Have available:

• Handwriting paper for each student.

Prepare:

• Handwriting lines on the chalkboard.

——— Lesson Content ———

Introduction

Relate the following information.

Woodcarving is one of the world's oldest arts. Hundreds of years ago, carved wooden blocks were used in India for decorating fabric, and books were printed in China from tablets of carved wood. In the Middle Ages, woodcarvers helped to decorate many beautiful churches. Early illustrations of the Scriptures were done by using pale brown ink on carved blocks of wood. Woodcuts and engravings

1. Man ypeop lewil ljud gey oubyt hewa yyo uwri te. *(Many people will judge you by the way you write.)*

2. Spa cingc anm akeab igdif fere ncei nho wyou rwor klo oks. *(Spacing can make a big difference in how your work looks.)*

3. Tr ywr iti ngwo rdsb ackw ard sfo rani ntere stin gcip her. *(Try writing words backwards for an interesting cipher.)*

Lesson 54   Written in Your Hearts   Worktext, page 66

Written in Your Hearts

name_____

Write the letters and words.

Handwriting Tips

Remember to proofread your work to check for mistakes.

ν ν

ν ν

veterinarian

χ χ

χ χ

xylographer

Write the verse on handwriting paper. Remember to proofread.

"But this shall be the covenant that I will make with the house of Israel: After those days, saith the Lord, I will put my law in their inward parts, and write it in their hearts; and will be their God, and they shall be my people."

Jeremiah 31:33

66   Use with Lesson 54.

Materials and Preparation

Have available:

- Handwriting paper for each student.

Prepare:

- Handwriting lines on the chalkboard.
- The following verse on the chalkboard (including the mistakes).

  And these uords, whech I comand thee this day, shall bee in thime hearl. Deuteromomy 6:6

— Lesson Content —

Introduction

Provide the following background.

The verse on our worktext page speaks of God's writing His commandments in the hearts of His people. There are several verses in the Old Testament that repeat this idea. Listen to Deuteronomy 6:6, 8: "And these words, which I command thee this day, shall be in thine heart. . . . And thou shalt bind them for a sign upon thine hand, and they shall be as frontlets between thine eyes." During the time of Christ, the Jewish people took this command literally. When a Jewish man went to morning prayers, he wore phylacteries, which were little boxes about 1½ inch square containing strips of Scripture verses. He tied one of these boxes onto his left arm and wore another one on his forehead.

Turn in your worktexts to page 66 and read the verse to yourselves. Do you think the Jews understood what God meant for them to do? What should they have done with God's commandments? What should we do? *(We should remember and obey them. Discuss as time permits.)*

Skill development

Focus on the handwriting tip on worktext page 66—Ask a student to read the handwriting tip at the top of the page. Remind the students that they should always proofread what they have written and correct any mistakes they find. Refer the students to the verse written on the chalkboard. Tell them to proofread it silently. Call on volunteers to rewrite parts of the verse, making the necessary corrections. Then direct a student to read aloud the corrected verse.

Guided practice

Focus on writing the letters *v* and *x*—Point out that uppercase *x* as well as lowercase *v* and *x* connect to letters that follow them and that both uppercase and lowercase *x* are crossed after the entire word is written. Instruct the students to practice the letters and words on the lines provided.

Guide the completion of worktext page 66—Direct a student to read aloud the verse. Remind the students to proofread their handwriting after they write the verse on handwriting paper.

Optional activity

Assign a Bible study—Instruct each student to read Deuteronomy 6:1-15 silently and write out the verses that tell the blessings (vv. 3, 10, 11) and punishment (v. 15) that God promised Israel in connection with His commandments.

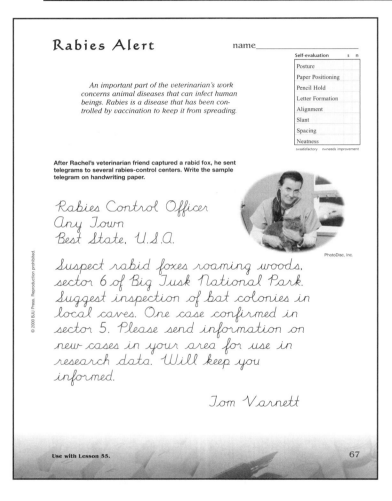

covered last weekend. "It sure is nice to live near a national park; there's plenty here to explore," she thought happily as she took a short cut through a small glade of ferns. She glimpsed the reddish-gold tail of a fox under the trees ahead and stopped short, expecting it to run away. When the fox did not move, she crept cautiously toward it, raising her camera. At the click of the camera shutter, the fox sprang toward her with a growl. Rachel jumped for a low-branched pine tree and reached the third limb with a single bound. She looked down. The fox stood in the ferns, still growling. When it finally trotted off into the trees, Rachel took the shortest way home, frowning as she puzzled over the fox's strange behavior. Right away, she phoned her friend, Tom Varnett, a veterinarian, and described what had happened. Later that night, Tom stopped by to tell Rachel that he had been able to catch the fox. He was pretty sure that it had rabies.

Direct attention to worktext page 67—Ask a student to read the paragraph at the top of the page. Explain that rabies is a virus that lives in the saliva of its host, which is why a person can get rabies from the bite of a rabid animal. Animals are also infected by breathing the air in caves where rabid bats live. Caution the students never to approach an animal that is behaving strangely.

Skill development

Review the formation of *v* and *x*—Direct several students to write the letters on the chalkboard as you verbalize the stroke descriptions. Ask the students how uppercase *v* is different from lowercase *v*, uppercase *x*, and lowercase *x*. *(It does not connect to letters that follow.)* Remind them that the letter *x* is crossed after the entire word is written. Allow volunteers to write the following words on the chalkboard.

    foxes   *caves*   *vaccination*

Assessment

Guide the completion of worktext page 67—Ask a student to read the directions. Then ask another student to read the telegram aloud. Direct the students to follow the format of the telegram on the page as they write the telegram on handwriting paper.

Materials and Preparation

Have available:

- Handwriting paper for each student.

Prepare:

- Handwriting lines on the chalkboard.

——— Lesson Content ———

Introduction

Read the following background story.

First thing after school, Rachel grabbed her camera and headed for the woods. Today she was hoping to get a good shot of the squirrel's nest she had dis-

Optional activity

Assign a book review—Ask each student to think about his favorite animal story. Have him write on handwriting paper a paragraph describing what happened in the story. For an additional paragraph he could tell why he liked that particular animal.

Lesson 56   Calligraphy Letters *p, g,* and *q*   Worktext, page 68

Calligraphy Letters

p, g, and *q*

name_____

Calligraphy Tips

Refer to the letter models on page 107 to help you avoid making letters that are too thin, too wide, too square, too sharp, or too curved.

Copy the practice strokes.

Write the letters *p, g,* and *q.*

Veterinarian
Xylographer
Watchmaker
Umpire

68   Use with Lesson 56.

© 2000 BJU Press. Reproduction prohibited.

Lesson Content

Introduction

Direct a warm-up activity—Direct the students to write three of each of the practice strokes on typing paper. Then direct them to write one letter that they have already learned (*all the lowercase letters but* j *and* y) on the clean side of the typing paper. Tell them to add eyes, a nose, a mouth, and some appendages (such as wings, arms, or legs). Finally, tell the students to name their "critter."

Skill development

Demonstrate the formation of lowercase *p, g,* and *q*— Write the letters on the lines on the overhead, verbalizing the direction of each stroke as you write. Show the students how the *g* and the *q* are formed similar to an *a* followed by different descender drops. Tell them to look at *p.* Ask them which letter has something in common with the *p.* (*the* q) Show the students that the last part of the *q* and the last part of the *p* are formed in the same way. Point out that all three letters reach almost to the descender line. Also mention that these letters should not connect to the letters that follow.

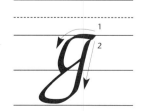

(1) Short diagonal right, Drop low.
(2) Swing around and lock.
(3) Cross right.

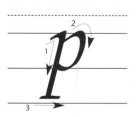

(1) Glide left and swing down to base line.
(2) Drop low, Glide left, Swing up right to lock.

Materials and Preparation

Have available:

- A chisel-point pen for each student.
- A guide sheet for each student.
- Two pieces of typing paper for each student.
- A transparency of the lowercase guide sheet.
- An overhead projector.
- An overhead pen.

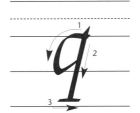

(1) Glide left,
    Swing around.
(2) Drop low.
(3) Cross right.

Guided practice

Direct handwriting on worktext page 68—Refer the students to the letter models on the lines at the bottom of the page. Remind them of the procedure for practicing the formation of the letters at the bottom of the page.

1. Note the arrow that indicates the direction of each stroke.

2. Trace the black letter with your finger.

3. Trace the gray letters with your pen.

Walk around the classroom to check that the students are making the correct strokes, both for practice strokes and for letter formation. Look for common errors.

Continued practice

Direct practice with typing paper and a guide sheet—Remind the students to use the side of the guide sheet labeled "Lowercase Guide Sheet." Tell each student to write the practice strokes and new letters *(p, g, and q)* and to review the letters that were taught in the last calligraphy lesson *(h and k)*.

Write the words *equip* and *plague* on the overhead for the students to see. Point out that these words will provide good review and practice in letter and word formation. Remind the students to leave the space of an *o* between words. Be sure to collect the pens when the students have finished.

Watchmaker and Umpire

The letters *w* and *u,* which have similar beginning strokes, will be reviewed in this unit in connection with the jobs of the watchmaker and umpire. The students will have an opportunity to exercise their ingenuity and demonstrate their knowledge of sports as they study these occupations.

Remember to look through the whole unit, giving special attention to the calligraphy lesson in the course of your preparation. As you practice faithfully, you too will become skilled in "beautiful writing."

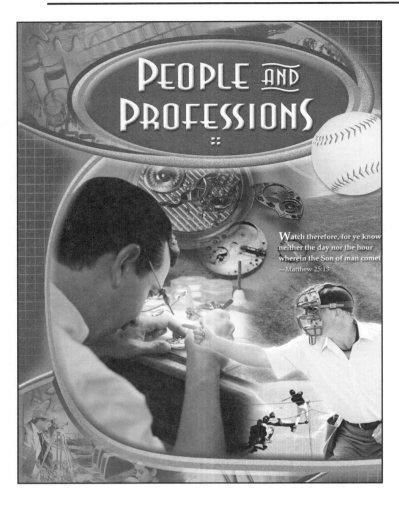

The Very Best   name_____

The Waltham Watch Company of Massachusetts was famous for its accurate pocket watches. Its pocket watches were adopted by the railroads because of their mechanical precision and durable casing.

Write the following advertisement on handwriting paper.

The Best in Railroad Watches In mint condition, this "Vanguard" pocket watch is stem-wound in a gold-filled railroad style case. 15 jewels. Circa 1918. A bargain at $900.

Write the check as Joe Wharton would write it to purchase the watch.

Joseph H. Wharton
Pine Mountain Place
Las Horas, CA

275

_____ ,20

67-1
532

Pay to the
Order of _____ $ _____

_____ Dollars

First Federal Bank

For _____

70   Use with Lesson 57.

Materials and Preparation

Have available:

- Handwriting paper for each student.

Prepare:

- Handwriting lines on the chalkboard.
- The following words on the chalkboard.

Joseph Wharton   watch   jewels

———— Lesson Content ————

Introduction

Introduce the unit—Tell the class to turn to worktext page 69 and read the unit verse silently. Ask them what they think the verse means. *(Answers will vary, but you should mention that we do not know when the Lord will return and that we should make sure that our lives are pleasing to Him so that we will not be ashamed when He does come back. BAT: 2c Faithfulness)*

Relate the following information.

How many of you have ever taken a clock or a watch apart to see how it is made? Did you notice the jewels in the watch movement? They can be made of glass, garnets, rubies, or sapphires, depending on the quality of the watch. The jewels are used in certain places inside the watch to reduce friction and to help the watch run better. Most wind-up watches today have at least a few jewels, and good quality watches have seventeen jewels. Complicated watches may have as many as twenty-three jewels.

Direct attention to worktext page 70—Explain that watches are often worn as jewelry and can be made with very lavish settings. Mention that the watch described on this page was housed in a plain gold case; the watch was expensive because of the high quality of its movement. If gems and other ornaments had been used to decorate the case, it would have cost even more. Ask a student to read the paragraph at the top of the page.

Skill development

Review the formation of *w*—Verbalize the direction of each stroke as you write the letters on the chalkboard. Point out that lowercase *w* connects to letters that follow but that uppercase *w* does not.

Swing up,
Drop and swing up,
Retrace and swing up.

Swing up,
Drop and swing up,
Retrace and swing up,
Sweep out.

Demonstrate writing the letter *w*—Point out the words on the chalkboard. Allow several students to write the words using your examples as models.

Demonstrate alternate styles of writing the letter *w* **(optional).**

Guided practice

Guide the completion of worktext page 70—Ask a student to read the advertisement in the middle of the page. Then direct attention to the sample check. Explain the different parts of the check to the students. Encourage them to write the correct information neatly on the check. Remind them to write the paragraph "The Best in Railroad Watches" on handwriting paper after completing the check.

Optional activity

Assign a designing activity—Ask each student to design and then describe a beautiful case for the pocket watch pictured on worktext page 70. Cases for these watches usually consisted of a round covering, hinged like a lid, that could be lifted up in order to look at the watch face. Ornamentation was done on the outside and the inside of this cover as well as around the edge of the watch itself. Gold, silver, or brass was generally used for the case, which was often encrusted with precious stones. The girls may want to use decorations of enameled (painted) flowers, vines, or angels. The boys may prefer engraved pictures of animals or designs with gold or silver studs, which look like small nail heads.

Call It!　　　　name_____

The umpire is an important part of baseball. His main job is to help a game go smoothly while keeping within the rules.

Listed below are several characteristics that some umpires have. Choose the seven good characteristics and write them on handwriting paper.

- is concerned for the safety of the players
- makes decisions calmly and firmly
- is courteous to the coach and players
- won't explain his calls
- gives his best effort
- has a neat appearance
- arrives late for a game
- knows the rules well
- makes calls in favor of the home team
- enjoys the sport

Use with Lesson 58.　　　71

© 2000 BJU Press. Reproduction prohibited.

Materials and Preparation

Have available:

- Handwriting paper for each student.

Prepare:

- Handwriting lines on the chalkboard.
- The following words on the chalkboard.

baseball	football	hockey
basketball	volleyball	soccer

——— Lesson Content ———

Introduction

Lead a game—Tell the students that each sport listed on the chalkboard makes use of one or more officials who see that the rules are followed. Ask which sport (or sports) fits with the following calls that an official could make.

1. "You're out!" *(baseball)*
2. "Defensive holding, number 27." *(football)*
3. "Net ball." *(volleyball)*

4. "Charging!" *(basketball, hockey)*
5. "Strike." *(baseball)*
6. "High sticking." *(hockey)*
7. "Offsides." *(soccer, football, hockey)*
8. "Pass interference." *(football)*
9. "Hands!" *(soccer)*
10. "Icing." *(hockey)*

Direct attention to worktext 71—Ask a student to read the paragraph at the top of the page.

Skill development

Review the formation of *u*—Verbalize the direction of each stroke as you write the letters on the chalkboard. Point out that both uppercase and lowercase *u* connect to letters that follow them.

Swing up,
Drop and swing up,
Retrace and curve.

Swing up,
Drop and swing up,
Retrace and curve.

Demonstrate the writing of the letter *u*—Write the following words on the chalkboard.

　　umpire　　　　*out*　　　　*rules*

Allow several students to write these words on the chalkboard, using your examples as models.

Demonstrate alternate styles of writing the letter *u* (optional).

Guided practice

Guide the completion of worktext page 71—Ask several students to read the directions and the list of characteristics. Discuss which characteristics are good ones. Instruct the students to write neatly as they write the seven good characteristics on handwriting paper.

Optional activity

Direct a donation—Ask each student to pick his favorite sport and pretend that he is going to donate to his school everything needed to pursue that sport. Ask him to make a list of all the items he will need to buy or build for the school.

Materials and Preparation

Have available:

- Handwriting paper for each student.

Prepare:

- The following words on the chalkboard.

alarm clock	wristwatch
sundial	digital clock
chronometer	grandfather clock
notched candle	clepsydra

——— Lesson Content ———

Introduction

Create interest in the lesson—Ask a student to read the list of timepieces on the chalkboard. Instruct the class to guess which one fits each description below.

1. This clock is worn on a band that fastens around the arm. *(wristwatch)*

2. As the hours pass, this timepiece burns down from one notch to another, showing the time. *(notched candle)*

3. This clock is usually enclosed in a large wooden case and has a pendulum as part of its mechanism. *(grandfather clock)*

4. The shadow cast by a vertical object is used to tell the time on this timepiece. *(sundial)*

5. Also called the Greek water clock, this timepiece consists of a container of water with a small hole in the bottom which allows the water to trickle out into a basin that is marked to show the hours. *(clepsydra)*

6. This timepiece does not have hands or a face; it has only numbers. *(digital clock)*

7. This exceptionally precise timepiece is often used on ships. *(chronometer)*

8. The bell or buzzer of this timepiece may sound at any hour. *(alarm clock)*

Skill development

Focus on the handwriting tip on worktext page 72—Ask a student to read aloud the handwriting tip at the top of the page. Direct attention to the two words written in the box. Emphasize that a mistake should be crossed out *neatly* so that attention is not drawn to the mistake.

Guided practice

Focus on writing the letters *w* and *u*—Direct attention to the model letters at the top of worktext page 72. Ask which letters connect to the letters that follow them. *(uppercase* u, *lowercase* w *and* u) Instruct the students to practice the letters and the words on the lines provided.

Direct the completion of worktext page 72—Call on volunteers to read the directions and the chart. Discuss what the Jews used to help them tell time. *(sun, dog barking, cock crowing, trumpet blasts)* Remind the students to write neatly and cross out any mistakes neatly as they write the chart on handwriting paper.

Optional activity

Direct an idiom study—Ask each student to write the meaning of the following "time" expressions as if he were explaining them to a new student who had just arrived in this country.

1. It's about time.

2. Time out.

3. The man lived in King David's time.

101

4. They're behind the times.

5. We had a good time.

6. He served time in prison.

7. My mother worked overtime.

8. What's the time?

9. She was always on time.

10. My dad ate a dozen cookies at a time.

Lesson 60   Close Game   Worktext, page 73

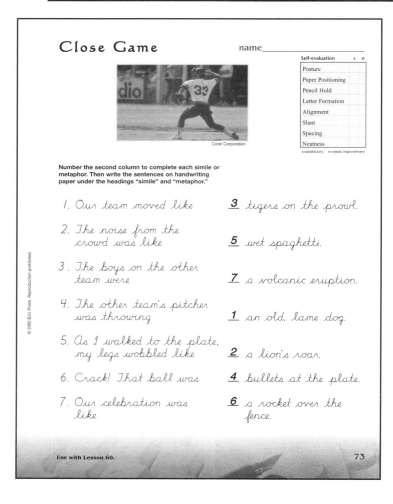

Close Game   name_____

Self-evaluation	s	n
Posture		
Paper Positioning		
Pencil Hold		
Letter Formation		
Alignment		
Slant		
Spacing		
Neatness		

Corel Corporation

s=satisfactory n=needs improvement

Number the second column to complete each simile or metaphor. Then write the sentences on handwriting paper under the headings "simile" and "metaphor."

1. Our team moved like   **3** tigers on the prowl.

2. The noise from the crowd was like   **5** wet spaghetti.

3. The boys on the other team were   **7** a volcanic eruption.

4. The other team's pitcher was throwing   **1** an old, lame dog.

5. As I walked to the plate, my legs wobbled like   **2** a lion's roar.

6. Crack! That ball was   **4** bullets at the plate.

7. Our celebration was like   **6** a rocket over the fence.

Use with Lesson 60.   73

© 2000 BJU Press. Reproduction prohibited.

simile—a comparison between unlike things that uses *as* or *like*. Example: *The waves were as big as mountains.*

metaphor—a comparison between unlike things that is implied rather than clearly stated. Example: *The waves were mountains crashing down upon me.*

Divide the class into two teams to compete in finishing the following sentences. For extra points they can tell whether each one is a simile or a metaphor.

1. I felt as scared as _____. *(simile)*

2. The snowflakes were _____. *(metaphor)*

3. The garden hose was a _____. *(metaphor)*

4. The tall buildings were like _____. *(simile)*

5. He ran like a _____. *(simile)*

6. The class was as quiet as _____. *(simile)*

7. The moon was _____. *(metaphor)*

Skill development

Review the formation of *u* and *w*—Allow several students to write the letters on the chalkboard as you verbalize the stroke descriptions. Ask which letter does not connect to the letters that follow. (*uppercase* w) Direct volunteers to write the following words on the chalkboard.

umpire	wobbled	Walt
bullet	prowl	

Assessment

Guide the completion of worktext page 74—Ask a student to read the instructions. Instruct the students to complete the matching of the similes and metaphors independently. When the students have finished the matching, ask several students to read the completed similes and metaphors. Direct the students to write the completed sentences on handwriting paper.

You may want to use the evaluation form in the Appendix with this lesson. Be aware that the back of this page will be used in the next lesson on calligraphy.

Materials and Preparation

Have available:

• Handwriting paper for each student.

Prepare:

• Handwriting lines on the chalkboard.

———— Lesson Content ————

Introduction

Conduct a review game—Remind the class of the difference between a simile and a metaphor, or write the following definitions on the chalkboard, leaving out key words.

102

Optional activity

Assign a news report—Instruct each student to reread the sentences on worktext page 73 and notice that the sentences outline a story about a baseball game. Ask him to rewrite the story as it might appear in a report on the sports page of his home newspaper.

Lesson 61   Calligraphy Letters *j* and *y*   Worktext, page 74

Calligraphy Letters
j and *y*   name_____

j y

Calligraphy Tips ●

Do not breathe! (At least not while making a stroke.)

Copy the practice strokes.

))))   ≋
((((≋

Write the letters *j* and *y*.

j j j

y y y

74   Use with Lesson 61.

© 2000 BJU Press. Reproduction prohibited.

——— Lesson Content ———

Introduction

Direct a warm-up activity—Direct the students to write three of each of the practice strokes on typing paper. Then direct them to write out a short sentence or Bible verse. Remind them to use only lowercase letters.

Skill development

Demonstrate the formation of lowercase *j* and *y*—Write the letters on the lines on the overhead, verbalizing the direction of each stroke as you write. Help the students to see that the *j* is similar to the first stroke of the *p* with the *dot* of the *i*. Direct their attention to the *y*. Point out that the *y* uses strokes similar to the *u* and a drop and a glide. Remind the students that they have produced all of the strokes necessary for the *j* and *y* and that formation of these letters should not present any problems. Point out that both letters reach almost to the descender line.

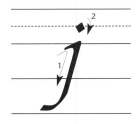

(1) Short diagonal right,
     Drop low and hook left.
(2) Dot.

Materials and Preparation

Have available:

- A chisel-point pen for each student.
- A guide sheet for each student.
- Two pieces of typing paper for each student.
- A transparency of the lowercase guide sheet.
- An overhead projector.
- An overhead pen.

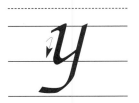

Short diagonal right,
Drop and swing right,
Push up to the body line,
Retrace,
Drop low and glide left.

Guided practice

Direct handwriting on worktext page 74—Point out that writing the practice strokes again will aid in better letter formation. Refer the students to the letter models on the lines at the bottom of the page. Remind them of the procedure for practicing the formation of the letters at the bottom of the page.

1. Note the arrow that indicates the direction of each stroke.
2. Trace the black letter with your finger.
3. Trace the gray letters with your pen.

Walk around the classroom to check that the students are making the correct strokes, both for practice strokes and for letter formation. Look for common errors.

Continued practice

Direct practice with typing paper and a guide sheet—Remind the students to use the side of the guide sheet labeled "Lowercase Guide Sheet." Tell each student to write the practice strokes and new letters (*y* and *j*), and to review the letters that were taught in the last calligraphy lesson (*p, g,* and *q*).

People and Professions

Yachtsman and Zoologist

In this unit, the exotic-sounding activities of the yachtsman and the zoologist provide a colorful background for the review of letters *y* and *z*.

Make sure that you preview the unit, paying special attention to the calligraphy lesson. Allow yourself plenty of practice time so that you will be well prepared to teach it.

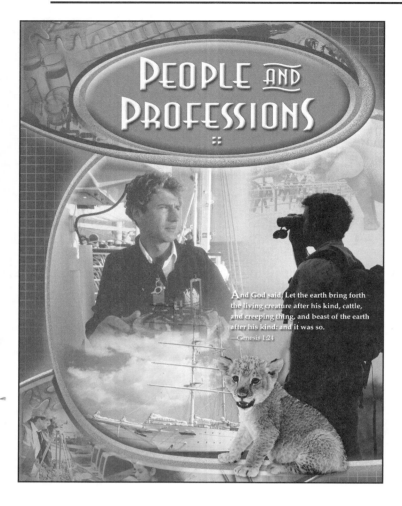

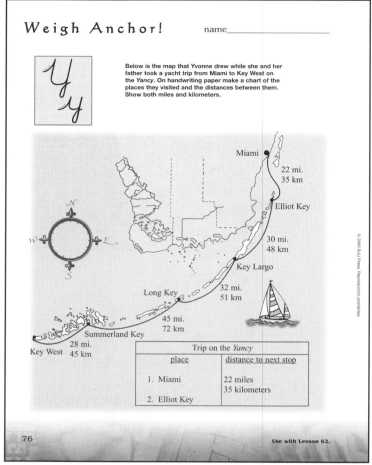

Weigh Anchor!   name_____

Below is the map that Yvonne drew while she and her father took a yacht trip from Miami to Key West on the *Yancy*. On handwriting paper make a chart of the places they visited and the distances between them. Show both miles and kilometers.

Miami

22 mi.
35 km

Elliot Key

30 mi.
48 km

Key Largo

32 mi.
51 km

Long Key

45 mi.
72 km

Summerland Key

Key West   28 mi.
45 km

Trip on the *Yancy*	
place	distance to next stop
1. Miami	22 miles 35 kilometers
2. Elliot Key	

76   **Use with Lesson 62.**

Materials and Preparation

Have available:

- Handwriting paper for each student.

Prepare:

- Handwriting lines on the chalkboard.

——— Lesson Content ———

Introduction

Introduce the unit—Ask a student to read the unit verse. Explain that *living creature* and *beast of the earth* are general terms for animals. *Cattle* includes such animals as cows, horses, sheep, and goats. *Creeping thing* refers to reptiles, insects, aquatic creatures, and small animals. The zoologist makes a scientific study of the vast array of animals that God has created. Point out that the yachtsman has opportunity to observe and appreciate many of the aquatic creatures. Mention that a yacht is any kind of small ship that is propelled by sails or a motor. It usually looks sleek and graceful.

Give background information about the metric system—Ask the class to tell you the name of the standard measuring system used by scientists all over the world. *(the metric system)* Relate that it was developed by a group of French scientists and adopted by France in 1799. Mention that the metric system is now common in most countries except the United States. It is a simple system to learn because all of its relationships are based on the decimal scale and the names it uses are all derived from the meter.

Introduce worktext page 76—Explain that Yvonne is a girl who has lived in Miami, Florida, for several years and enjoys yachting with her father. He named their yacht the *Yancy* for Yvonne and her mother, Nancy. When Yvonne's aunt invited them down to Key West, they decided to travel by yacht and visit several of the Florida Keys on the way. (A key is a reef or small coral islet; most often the word refers to the series of low islands off the coast of Florida.) The map on worktext page 76 shows their trip.

Skill development

Review the formation of *y*—Verbalize the direction of each stroke as you write the letters on the chalkboard. Point out that the lowercase and uppercase letters are similar in appearance and that both connect to letters that follow them.

Swing up,
Drop and swing up,
Retrace,
Drop low and loop.

Swing up,
Drop and swing up,
Retrace,
Drop low and loop.

Demonstrate the writing of the letter *y*—Write the following words on the chalkboard.

Yvonne   *yacht*   *key*

Allow several students to write these words on the chalkboard, using your examples as models.

Demonstrate alternate styles of writing the letter *y* (optional).

Guided practice

Guide the completion of worktext page 76—Use the map on the worktext page as you lead a discussion of the stops Yvonne and her father made during their yacht trip from Miami to Key West. Direct attention to the chart. Choose a volunteer to read the first entry on the chart. Instruct the students to write on handwriting paper the heading and the first entry on the chart and then to complete the chart independently.

Optional activity

Direct a dictionary activity—Instruct each student to look up the word *key* in a dictionary and choose six definitions to write on handwriting paper. (Some dictionaries have more than ten entries for this word.)

Then and Now　　name_____

The main objective of a zoologist is to understand the lives of animals. His work may range from studying a dog's brain cells to reporting on the behavior of giraffes in Africa. Many of the discoveries made by zoologists have given medical researchers valuable information about the human body.

Write the outline below on handwriting paper.

Zoology
I. Ancient collections of animals
    A. Chinese and Egyptian
    B. King Solomon's
II. Scientific study of animals
    A. Books by Aristotle
    B. Animals from other lands
    C. Experiments with animal anatomy
III. Zoology today
    A. Many branches of study
    B. Many careers to choose from

Use with Lesson 63.　　77

Materials and Preparation

Have available:

- Handwriting paper for each student.

Prepare:

- Handwriting lines on the chalkboard.

—— Lesson Content ——

Introduction

Lead a note-taking activity—Explain that you will read an article about zoology. Ask the students to listen carefully for the main points in each of the three paragraphs you read and to take notes. If necessary, review outline form on the chalkboard. (Use Roman numerals for headings and uppercase letters for subheadings.) Choose one of the following procedures (depending on the experience your class has had with taking notes).

1. Tell the students to listen while you read the article. Discuss the main points that they heard if it seems necessary. Read the article again and have them take notes.

2. Have the students take notes as you read the article. If necessary, read it a second time so that they can revise their notes.

Read the following article on zoology.

Man has had collections of animals ever since ancient times. The Chinese and the Egyptians kept exotic animals in their palaces, and King Solomon had a world-famous collection of captive wild animals.

The scientific study of animals developed gradually. One of the first zoologists was Aristotle, who lived in Greece more than three hundred years before Christ. He wrote several books about animals and their structure. His work encouraged the systematic study of living things. Later on, new animals were studied when explorers from Europe visited other continents and brought back strange wild creatures. The invention of the microscope in following years led to the discovery of tiny forms of life that no one knew anything about. Scientists then began to study the anatomy of animals to learn about organs that were similar in both human and animal bodies. William Harvey, for example, was able to demonstrate the function of the heart, arteries, and veins because of his experiments with animals.

Zoology has changed greatly since Aristotle's time. It has become a broad science with many branches. Today, a person who wants to become a zoologist will find that he needs to specialize in one area. He may decide to study birds, insects, animal body tissues, animal environments, or one of a dozen other fields. There are many careers open to a zoologist. He may work at a wildlife preserve, a museum, or a zoo. He could get a job with the federal government, conduct expeditions, or do various types of research. No matter what work he chooses, the zoologist makes an important contribution to helping us understand and improve our world.

Direct attention to worktext page 77—Ask a student to read the paragraph at the top of the page. Explain that this page is an example of notes that could be written about the article just read.

Skill development

Review the formation of *z*—Verbalize the direction of each stroke as you write the letters on the chalkboard. Point out that uppercase and lowercase *z* connect to letters that follow them. Discuss the similarities between uppercase and lowercase *z*.

Swing up,
Curve around and down
to six,
Drop low and loop.

Swing up,
Curve around and down
to six,
Drop low and loop.

Demonstrate the writing of lowercase *z* **in pairs**—Write *z* in pairs on the chalkboard as the students air-trace the letters. Allow several students to come to the chalkboard to write the following words.

buzz   fuzzy   pizza

Demonstrate alternate styles of writing the letter *z* **(optional).**

Guided practice

Guide the completion of worktext page 77—Call on students to read the notes they took about zoology at the beginning of the lesson. Instruct the students to compare the notes on the worktext page with their own notes as they write the sample notes on handwriting paper.

Optional activity

Direct a classifying activity—Tell each student to pretend that he is a zoologist visiting an island that is inhabited by some very unusual animals. He is to make a chart that classifies the animals he encounters by describing them under these six headings: the animal's name, its color(s), the sound it makes, the number of appendages that it has (legs, trunk, tail, etc.), its facial details, and its habitat.

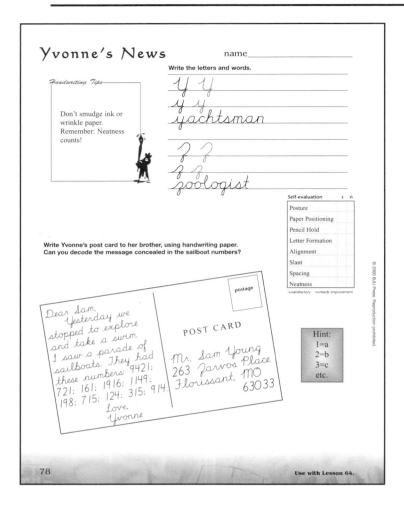

Review the formation of *y* and *z*—Direct several students to write the letters on the chalkboard as you verbalize the stroke descriptions. Ask the students how the letters are similar. *(The uppercase and lowercase letters are similar; all the letters connect to letters that follow them.)*

Allow volunteers to write the following words on the chalkboard.

zero   Yancy   yesterday   Zarvos

Guided practice

Focus on writing the letters *y* and *z*—Direct attention to the model letters at the top of worktext page 78. Instruct the students to practice the letters and words on the lines provided.

Assessment

Guide the completion of worktext page 78—Ask a student to read the post card that Yvonne wrote to Sam. Reassure the students that decoding Yvonne's puzzle is not part of the assessment. Tell them that if they try to decode the message, they will find that one-digit and two-digit numerals are combined to make the code more difficult. Instruct them to write Yvonne's note first and then Sam's address as they write the post card on handwriting paper. Remind the students to write neatly and then to complete the self-evaluation form on worktext page 78.

You may want to use the evaluation form in the Appendix with this lesson. Be aware that the back of this page will be used in the next lesson on calligraphy

Answer key:
9 4 2 1: 7 2 1: 1 6 1: 1 9 1 6: 1 1 4 9: 1 9 8: 7 1 5: 1 2 4:
i d u g u   p a s   p a n i s h g o   l d

3 1 5: 9 1 4
c o i n

I dug up a Spanish gold coin.

Optional activity

Direct a letter-writing activity—Tell each student to use handwriting paper to write a letter to a friend about a real or imaginary trip he has taken.

Materials and Preparation

Have available:

- Handwriting paper for each student.

Prepare:

- Handwriting lines on the chalkboard.

——— Lesson Content ———

Introduction

Create interest in the lesson—Tell the class that Yvonne and her brother enjoy writing letters to each other in code. Ask if anyone has ever written coded messages. Allow a short time for discussion before directing attention to the top of worktext page 78.

Skill development

Focus on the handwriting tip on worktext page 78—Choose a student to read aloud the handwriting tip at the top of the page. Emphasize the importance of neat, legible handwriting.

Words to Work By

"The door to the room of success swings on the hinges of opposition."

"The test of your character is what it takes to stop you."

"You can do anything you ought to do."

"Blessed is the man who knows how to make stepping stones out of stumbling stones."

—taken from "Chapel Sayings of Dr. Bob Jones Sr."

Use with Lesson 1.

Post-Test

name_____

Write the quotations from page iv.

When finally the lesson they learn,
Back home they decided to return,
But imagine their glee
When, approaching, they see
That their living as scribes they can earn!

Use with Lesson 65.   79

Materials and Preparation

Have available:

- The students' pretests from Lesson 1.

Prepare:

- Handwriting lines on the chalkboard.

—— Lesson Content ——

Introduction

Direct attention to worktext page 79—Ask a student to read the limerick. Discuss why Penfellow and Chanticleer returned home and why they were happy when they arrived.

Lead a review—Direct the students to list the people and professions about which they have learned during handwriting time. Allow them to look at the table of contents in the worktext to refresh their memories. Ask volunteers to write on the chalkboard the profession that represents each letter of the alphabet.

Post-test

Direct a post-test—Help the students to recall the specific people they have studied and their professions. Remind the students that we remember these people for their work and determination. (BAT: 2e Work) Ask a student to read the directions on worktext page 79. Allow volunteers to read the quotations about work and determination on worktext page iv. Then instruct the students to use page iv as a guide as they complete page 79 independently, using their best handwriting.

Guide the students in contrasting the pretest and the post-test—Before collecting the papers, distribute the pretests and encourage each student to note his own improvement in handwriting.

Optional activity

Direct a writing-and-acting activity—Tell each student to use handwriting paper to describe the profession or person he found most interesting. Then allow each student to dramatize the profession or person about whom he wrote.

PEOPLE AND PROFESSIONS

Character Quality

As the students learn the uppercase calligraphy letters in this unit, they will be writing words that describe Christian character traits. While they are studying traits that contribute to "character quality," they should also strive to write "quality characters."

Make sure that you preview the unit, paying close attention to the lessons on spacing and layout. Allow class time in your schedule for the students to copy one of the examples at the end of the student worktext and to design a piece of calligraphy of their own.

Lesson 66   Calligraphy Lowercase Review   Worktext, pages 81-83

Materials and Preparation

Have available:

- A chisel-point pen for each student.
- A guide sheet for each student.
- A piece of typing paper for each student.

- A transparency of the advanced guide sheet.
- An overhead projector.
- An overhead pen.

> You have been using the guide sheet for lowercase letters. Now you will need the advanced guide sheet for uppercase letters.

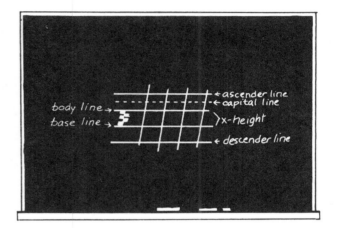

——— Lesson Content ———

Introduction

Explain the purpose of this lesson—Congratulate the students on having completed the entire lowercase letters of the alphabet. Explain that this is not the end of calligraphy lessons but only the end of the formal presentation of the lowercase letters. Point out the verse on page 81. Tell them that following this review is a section for uppercase Chancery cursive letters and numerals. Point out that although they will produce a complete sentence today, they will not be using uppercase letters since they have not learned them yet.

Calligraphy Lowercase Review

a b c d e f g h i j

k l m n o p q r

s t u v w x y z

Now Penfellow's speed is much greater,
And his puppet's a good illustrator;
For with nothing to view
(And much writing to do),
The two scribes must do daydreaming later.

Calligraphy Tips

Leave an adequate amount of space between lines so that your work is readable.

Write the following on the lines on page 83.

travelling beneath
the azure sky in
our jolly ox-cart,
we often hit
bumps quite hard

82   Use with Lesson 66.

Use with Lesson 66.   83

Introduce the advanced guide sheet—Hold up a guide sheet so that the side labeled "Advanced Guide Sheet" faces the students. Indicate the five guidelines—the ascender, capital, body, base, and descender lines. Remind the students to go beyond the capital line almost to the ascender line on tall letters. Tell them that they will not use the capital line until the next lesson. Finally, show the students where the x-height is located in relation to the other lines.

Skill development

Remind the students of the proper positions that they have learned—Remind them of the tips about proper body position, paper position, pen hold, and pen angle.

Direct a warm-up activity—After distributing a piece of typing paper and a pen to each student, direct the class to write five of each practice stroke.

Guided practice

Direct handwriting on worktext pages 82 and 83—Ask a student to read the limerick at the top of page 82. Read the calligraphy tip at the top of the page. Refer the students to the letter models at the top of page 82; then direct them to look carefully at the sentence. Point out letter spacing and word spacing. Tell the students to read the sentence so that they see it as a unit and not just a grouping of letters that happen to form words. Then direct the students to write the phrase from page 82 on the lines on page 83. Collect page 83 from each student and write comments on the pages.

The back of worktext page 83 will be used in the next lesson.

114

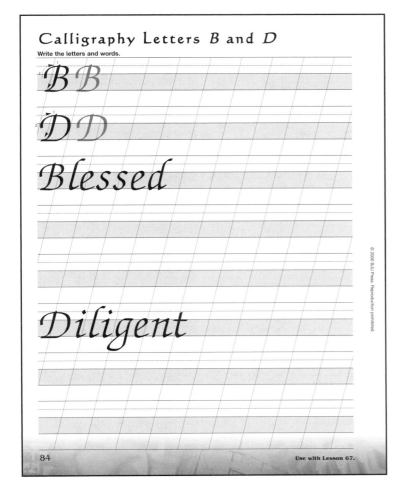

Calligraphy Letters *B* and *D*

Write the letters and words.

B B

D D

Blessed

Diligent

84   Use with Lesson 67.

© 2000 BJU Press. Reproduction prohibited.

Materials and Preparation

Have available:

- A chisel-point pen for each student.
- A guide sheet for each student.
- Two pieces of typing paper for each student.
- A transparency of the advanced guide sheet.
- An overhead projector.
- An overhead pen.
- A Bible.
- Worktext page 84 for each student.

You may prefer not to collect the calligraphy pens after each lesson since the students will be using them for all lessons now.

— Lesson Content —

Introduction

Lead a word study—Explain to the students that each of the next calligraphy lessons will highlight certain character qualities. Ask a student to read Psalm 1:1-2. Point out the word *blessed* and tell the class that this is one of the qualities for this lesson. Ask them if they fulfill the requirements in this verse for being blessed. Tell the class that the other character quality is *diligent*. Ask what *diligent* means. *(persevering, hard-working, industrious)* Challenge them to make sure that this quality describes the way they practice calligraphy.

Introduce the students to uppercase Chancery cursive letters—Tell the students that the capital letters are called uppercase because they were stored in the top drawer of the printer's chest of drawers—the upper case. Give the two following reasons that uppercase Chancery cursive letters are a little more difficult to form than lowercase letters.

1. Uppercase letters are larger than lowercase letters, and that means that more time, concentration, and breath control are needed to form these letters.
2. Uppercase letters are not used as often as lowercase letters.

Also point out that uppercase letters go only as high as the capital line because if they reached as high as the ascender line, they would "overpower" the lowercase letters.

Skill development

Direct a warm-up activity—After distributing a piece of typing paper and a pen to each student, direct the class to write five of each practice stroke.

Demonstrate the formation of uppercase *B* and *D*—Write the letters on the lines on the overhead, using the transparency guide and verbalizing the direction of each stroke as you write. Point out that the first stroke and part of the second stroke of the letters *B* and *D* are alike.

(1) Drop and slight curve left.
(2) Swing left and up, Glide right, around, and down to lock, Retrace, around, and down to lock.

115

(1) Drop and slight curve left.
(2) Swing left and up, Glide right, around, and down to lock,

Guided practice

Direct handwriting on worktext page 84—Point out the arrow that indicates the direction of each stroke. Direct the students to read the directions and complete the page.

Walk around the classroom to check that the students are making the correct strokes for the letters. Look for common errors.

Continued practice

Direct practice with typing paper and a guide sheet—Tell the students to use the advanced guide sheet as they practice the new letters and words on typing paper.

Direct a special activity—Tell the students that sometimes an artist chooses to make the first letter of the first word (or an entire word) larger for emphasis. Direct them to design a special *B*.

Be merciful unto me, O God: be merciful unto me: for my soul trusteth in thee:

Lesson 68   Calligraphy Letters *C* and *G*

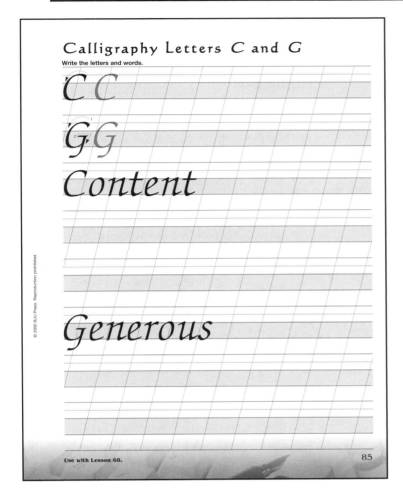

Calligraphy Letters *C* and *G*

Write the letters and words.

C C

G G

Content

Generous

© 2000 BJU Press. Reproduction prohibited.

Use with Lesson 68.   85

Materials and Preparation

Have available:

- A chisel-point pen for each student.
- A guide sheet for each student.
- Two pieces of typing paper for each student.
- A transparency of the advanced guide sheet.
- An overhead projector.
- An overhead pen.
- A Bible.

—— Lesson Content ——

Introduction

Lead a word study—Ask a student to read Hebrews 13:5. When he is finished, repeat the words *and be content*. Tell the students that being content is one of the character qualities for this lesson. Help the class to deduce from the verse why we can be content. *(because we have Jesus, who can fill all our needs)* Mention that the other character quality is being generous. Ask three students to give a synonym for this trait. *(liberal, big-hearted, kind, bountiful)*

Review the terms related to the advanced guide sheet—Ask a student to indicate and name the five guidelines on the guide sheet. Remind the students that the uppercase letters should reach only as high as the capital line.

Skill development

Direct a warm-up activity—After distributing a piece of typing paper and a pen to each student, direct the class to write five of each practice stroke.

Demonstrate the formation of uppercase *C* and *G*—Write the letters on the lines on the overhead, using the transparency guide and verbalizing the direction of each stroke as you write. Point out that the stroke of *C* and the first stroke of *G* are identical.

Glide left,
Swing around.

(1) Glide left,
*   Swing around.*
(2) Glide right,
*   Drop low and hook.*

Guided practice

Direct handwriting on worktext page 85—Direct the students to remove page 85 from their worktexts. Point out the arrow that indicates the direction of each stroke. Direct them to read the directions and complete the page.

Walk around the classroom to check that the students are making the correct strokes for the letters. Look for common errors.

Continued practice

Direct practice with typing paper and a guide sheet—Tell the students to use the advanced guide sheet as they practice the new letters and words on typing paper.

The back of this page will be used in the next lesson.

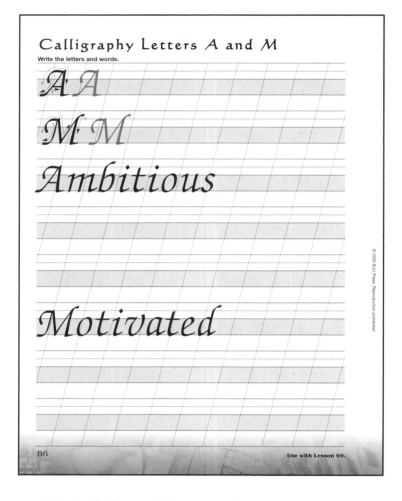

Materials and Preparation

Have available:

- A chisel-point pen for each student.
- A guide sheet for each student.
- Two pieces of typing paper for each student.
- A transparency of the advanced guide sheet.
- An overhead projector.
- An overhead pen.
- A Bible.
- Worktext page 86 for each student.

——— Lesson Content ———

Introduction

Lead a word study—Ask the students whether it is a good thing to be ambitious. Explain that *ambitious* means "eager for success." Help them to understand that whether ambition is good or not depends on the reason for it. Does the person want to be successful for himself or for God's glory? Tell them that this character quality is related to the second one for the lesson: *motivated.* Ask a student to read

Matthew 28:19-20; then ask a volunteer to tell how these verses can motivate us to tell others about Christ. *(Jesus commands us, and He promises to be with us.)*

Skill development

Direct a warm-up activity—After distributing a piece of typing paper and a pen to each student, direct the class to write five of each practice stroke.

Demonstrate the formation of uppercase *A* and *M*— Write the letters on the lines on the overhead, using the transparency guide and verbalizing the direction of each stroke as you write. Point out that the *M* is similar to two *A*'s. Point out that these two letters are a little difficult to form because the verticals do not follow the 13° letter slant, but the overall effect of the letter must be that of one that does follow the 13° slant.

(1) Drop left and glide left.
(2) Swing left and glide right,
    Drop and glide right.
(3) Cross.

(1) Drop left and glide left.
(2) Swing left and glide right,
    Drop right,
    Climb right to capital line.
(3) Start high, glide left, and drop to base line.
    Glide right.

Guided practice

Direct handwriting on worktext page 86—Point out the arrow that indicates the direction of each stroke. Direct the students to read the directions and complete the page.

Walk around the classroom to check that the students are making the correct strokes for the letters. Look for common errors.

Continued practice

Direct practice with typing paper and a guide sheet— Tell the students to use the advanced guide sheet as they practice the new letters and words on typing paper.

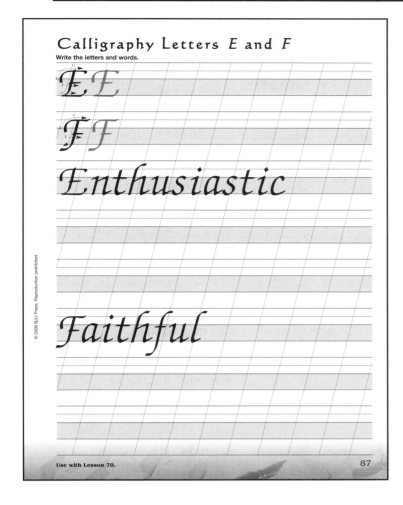

Skill development

Direct a warm-up activity—After distributing a piece of typing paper and a pen to each student, direct the class to write five of each practice stroke.

Demonstrate the formation of uppercase *E* and *F*— Write the letters on the lines on the overhead, using the transparency guide and verbalizing the direction of each stroke as you write. Point out that the *F* is similar to the *E*.

(1) Drop and curve left, Retrace, glide right and curve up.
(2) Swing left and glide right and curve down.
(3) Cross.

(1) Drop and glide left.
(2) Swing left and glide right and slight curve up.
(3) Cross.

Materials and Preparation

Have available:

- A chisel-point pen for each student.
- A guide sheet for each student.
- Two pieces of typing paper for each student.
- A transparency of the advanced guide sheet.
- An overhead projector.
- An overhead pen.

—— Lesson Content ——

Introduction

Lead a word study—Ask a student to tell what *enthusiastic* means. *(full of excitement or great interest)* Then ask the class why it is important for a Christian to be enthusiastic. *(It will bring glory to God, our work will be better, and the unsaved will be favorably impressed.)* Mention that the second character trait, *faithful,* is important for the same reason. Ask two students to give a specific example of how enthusiasm or faithfulness can bring glory to God.

Guided practice

Direct handwriting on worktext page 87—Direct the students to remove page 87 from their worktexts. Point out the arrow that indicates the direction of each stroke. Direct them to read the directions and complete the page.

Walk around the classroom to check that the students are making the correct strokes for the letters. Look for common errors.

Continued practice

Direct practice with typing paper and a guide sheet— Tell the students to use the advanced guide sheet as they practice the new letters and words on typing paper.

The back of this page will be used in the next lesson.

Materials and Preparation

Have available:

- A chisel-point pen for each student.
- A guide sheet for each student.
- Two pieces of typing paper for each student.
- A transparency of the advanced guide sheet.
- An overhead projector.
- An overhead pen.
- A Bible.
- Worktext page 88 for each student.

—— Lesson Content ——

Introduction

Direct a Bible study—Tell the class that the character traits for this lesson are sometimes considered by the world to be signs of weakness. However, that is not God's opinion of them. Ask a student to read aloud I Peter 5:5; then ask the students to guess the trait. *(humble)* Repeat this procedure with Ephesians 4:32 for *kind*. Point out that both of

these verses are phrased as a command. Remind the students that God never gives a command without enabling us to obey it.

Skill development

Direct a warm-up activity—After distributing a piece of typing paper and a pen to each student, direct the class to write five of each practice stroke.

Demonstrate the formation of uppercase *H* and *K*—Write the letters on the lines on the overhead, using the transparency guide and verbalizing the direction of each stroke as you write. Point out that the cross of the *H* and the point at which the second stroke of the *K* touches the first stroke are both below the body line. But the second stroke of the *H* starts above the uppercase line.

(1) Swing left and around,
    Drop and glide left.
(2) Start high,
    Glide left,
    Drop and glide right.
(3) Cross.

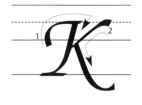

(1) Swing left and glide
    right,
    Drop and glide left,
    Retrace and glide right.
(2) Slight glide left,
    Drop left,
    Drop right low and
    curve.

Guided practice

Direct handwriting on worktext page 88—Point out the arrow that indicates the direction of each stroke. Direct the students to read the directions and complete the page.

Walk around the classroom to check that the students are making the correct strokes for the letters. Look for common errors.

Continued practice

Direct practice with typing paper and a guide sheet—Tell the students to use the advanced guide sheet as they practice the new letters and words on typing paper.

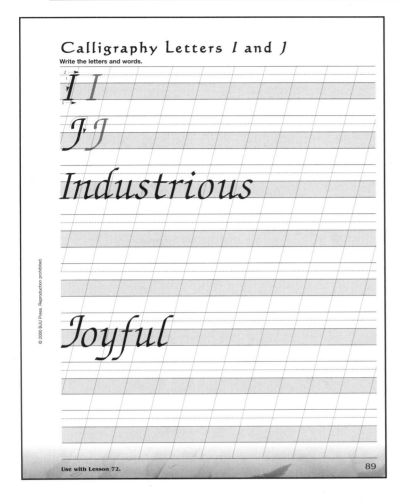

Calligraphy Letters *I* and *J*
Write the letters and words.

I I

J J

Industrious

Joyful

Use with Lesson 72.   89

© 2000 BJU Press. Reproduction prohibited.

Demonstrate the formation of uppercase *I* and *J*—Write the letters on the lines on the overhead, using the transparency guide and verbalizing the direction of each stroke as you write.

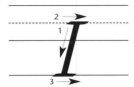

(1) Drop.
(2) Cross right at the top.
(3) Cross right at the
bottom.

Swing up and around,
Drop and hook left.

Guided practice

Direct handwriting on worktext page 89—Direct the students to remove page 89 from their worktexts. Point out the arrow that indicates the direction of each stroke. Direct them to read the directions and complete the page.

Continued practice

Direct practice with typing paper and a guide sheet—Tell the students to use the advanced guide sheet as they practice the new letters and words on typing paper.

The back of this page will be used in the next lesson.

Materials and Preparation

Have available:

- A chisel-point pen for each student.
- A guide sheet for each student.
- Two pieces of typing paper for each student.
- A transparency of the advanced guide sheet.
- An overhead projector.
- An overhead pen.

——— Lesson Content ———

Introduction

Lead a song—The character traits for this lesson are *industrious* and *joyful*. Mention this and then lead the class in singing "There Is Joy in Serving Jesus."

Skill development

Direct a warm-up activity—After distributing a piece of typing paper and a pen to each student, direct the class to write five of each practice stroke.

Skill development

Direct a warm-up activity—After distributing a piece of typing paper and a pen to each student, direct the class to write five of each practice stroke.

Demonstrate the formation of uppercase _L_ and _S_—Write the letters on the lines on the overhead, using the transparency guide and verbalizing the direction of each stroke as you write. Point out that the uppercase _S_ is identical to its "little brother," lowercase _s_.

Glide left,
Drop and glide left,
Retrace, glide right and
*   hook.*

Swing up to left,
Swerve around and back
*   to the left.*

Materials and Preparation

Have available:

- A chisel-point pen for each student.
- A guide sheet for each student.
- Two pieces of typing paper for each student.
- A transparency of the advanced guide sheet.
- An overhead projector.
- An overhead pen.
- A Bible.
- Worktext page 90 for each student.

———— Lesson Content ————

Introduction

Lead a discussion—The two character traits presented in this lesson, _loyal_ and _Spirit-filled,_ are related in that when we let the Holy Spirit rule our hearts, we will be loyal to the right person or idea. Discuss this briefly after reading Romans 8:13-14 aloud.

Guided practice

Direct handwriting on worktext page 90—Point out the arrow that indicates the direction of each stroke. Direct the students to read the directions and complete the page.

Continued practice

Direct practice with typing paper and a guide sheet—Tell the students to use the advanced guide sheet as they practice the new letters and words on typing paper.

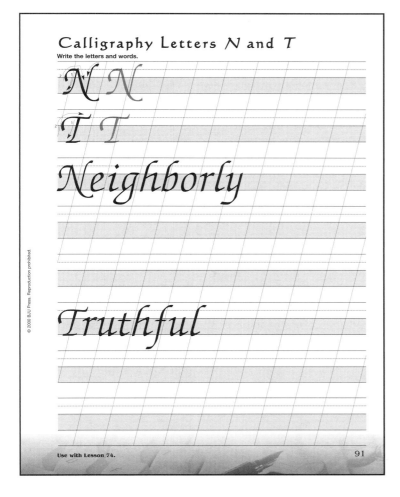

Calligraphy Letters N and T
Write the letters and words.

N N

T T

Neighborly

Truthful

Use with Lesson 74.   91

Materials and Preparation

Have available:

- A chisel-point pen for each student.
- A guide sheet for each student.
- Two pieces of typing paper for each student.
- A transparency of the advanced guide sheet.
- An overhead projector.
- An overhead pen.
- A Bible.

—— Lesson Content ——

Introduction

Direct a word search—Ask volunteers to read Galatians 5:14 and Ephesians 4:25 to the class. Mention that one of the character traits for this lesson begins with an *n* and the other begins with a *t*. Have the class guess the traits *neighborly* and *truthful* from the verses they hear.

Skill development

Direct a warm-up activity—After distributing a piece of typing paper and a pen to each student, direct the class to write five of each practice stroke.

Demonstrate the formation of uppercase *N* and *T*— Write the letters on the lines on the overhead, using the transparency guide and verbalizing the direction of each stroke as you write. Point out that there are no similarities between *N* and *T*. Show the students that the first stroke of the *N* is identical to that of the *H*.

(1) *Drop and glide left.*
(2) *Swing up and around,*
    Drop right low and
        curve right.
(3) *Start high,*
    Glide left and drop to
        lock.

(1) *Swing left and up,*
    Glide right,
    Hook up.
(2) *Drop and glide left,*
    Retrace and glide right.

Guided practice

Direct handwriting on worktext page 91—Direct the students to remove page 91 from their worktexts. Point out the arrow that indicates the direction of each stroke. Ask them to read the directions and complete the page.

Continued practice

Direct practice with typing paper and a guide sheet— Tell the students to use the advanced guide sheet as they practice the new letters and words on typing paper.

The back of this page will be used in the next lesson.

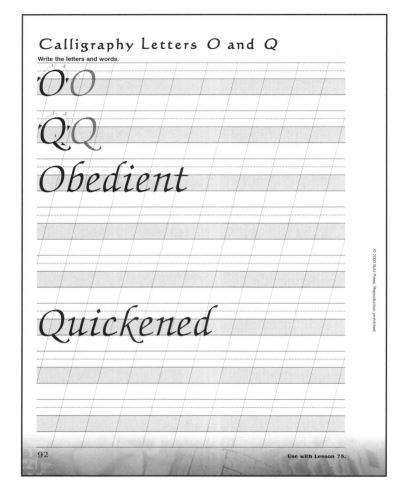

quickened; those who obey the gospel's command to believe will also be quickened.)

Skill development

Direct a warm-up activity—After distributing a piece of typing paper and a pen to each student, direct the class to write five of each practice stroke.

Demonstrate the formation of uppercase *Q* and *O*— Write the letters on the lines on the overhead, using the transparency guide and verbalizing the direction of each stroke as you write. Point out that uppercase *Q* and *O* are both identical to lowercase *o* except that they are larger.

Point out to the students that if they form the *o* shape for these letters in a box, the first stroke begins in the upper right-hand corner of the box and ends in the bottom left-hand corner. Warn the students that while forming the last part of the third stroke of the letter *Q* they should keep the drop right very straight until the slight curve at the end.

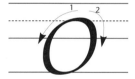

(1) Swing around left.
(2) Swing around right.

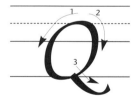

(1) Swing around left.
(2) Swing around right.
(3) Drop right and curve.

Materials and Preparation

Have available:

- A chisel-point pen for each student.
- A guide sheet for each student.
- Two pieces of typing paper for each student.
- A transparency of the advanced guide sheet.
- An overhead projector.
- An overhead pen.
- Worktext page 92 for each student.

———— Lesson Content ————

Introduction

Direct a discussion—Make sure that the class understands the meaning of the character trait *quickened. (to make alive, stimulate)* Point out that the Holy Spirit quickened Christians from the dead in the spiritual sense and will someday quicken Christians from the dead in a physical sense. Tell the class that the other character trait is *obedient.* Ask the students if they can think of a connection between the two. *(Christians who obey the Holy Spirit will be*

Guided practice

Direct handwriting on worktext page 92—Point out the arrow that indicates the direction of each stroke. Direct the students to read the directions and complete the page.

Continued practice

Direct practice with typing paper and a guide sheet— Tell the students to use the advanced guide sheet as they practice the new letters and words on typing paper.

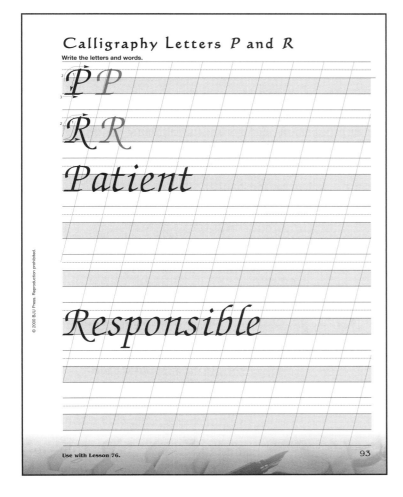

Calligraphy Letters *P* and *R*

Write the letters and words.

P P

R R

Patient

Responsible

Use with Lesson 76.   93

Materials and Preparation

Have available:

- A chisel-point pen for each student.
- A guide sheet for each student.
- Two pieces of typing paper for each student.
- A transparency of the advanced guide sheet.
- An overhead projector.
- An overhead pen.

—— Lesson Content ——

Introduction

Direct a word study—Tell the class that the two character traits for this lesson are *patient* and *responsible*. Mention that these are especially hard qualities to develop. Elicit the meaning of each trait. *(patient—enduring trouble or hardship without complaining; responsible—dependable or trustworthy)* Ask the students for their ideas about how to become more patient and/or trustworthy. *(Ask God to help them practice patience and responsibility when the opportunities come along.)*

Skill development

Direct a warm-up activity—After distributing a piece of typing paper and a pen to each student, direct the class to write five of each practice stroke.

Demonstrate the formation of uppercase *P* and *R*— Write the letters on the lines on the overhead, using the transparency guide and verbalizing the direction of each stroke as you write. Point out that the first stroke of the uppercase *R* is just like the first stroke of the *T* with the exception that the glide is shorter. Also point out that the first part of the second stroke of both letters is like the *B* and *D*. Direct the students to note that the lock of the second stroke is just below the body line. Finally, point out that the drop of the *R* is to be straight until the curve.

(1) Drop.
(2) Swing left and around
    to lock.
(3) Cross at the bottom.

(1) Drop and glide left,
    Retrace and glide right.
(2) Swing left and around
    to lock,
    Drop right low and
    curve.

Guided practice

Direct handwriting on worktext page 93—Direct the students to remove page 93 from their worktexts. Point out the arrow that indicates the direction of each stroke. Direct them to read the directions and complete the page.

Continued practice

Direct practice with typing paper and a guide sheet— Tell the students to use the advanced guide sheet as they practice the new letters and words on typing paper.

The back of this page will be used in the next lesson.

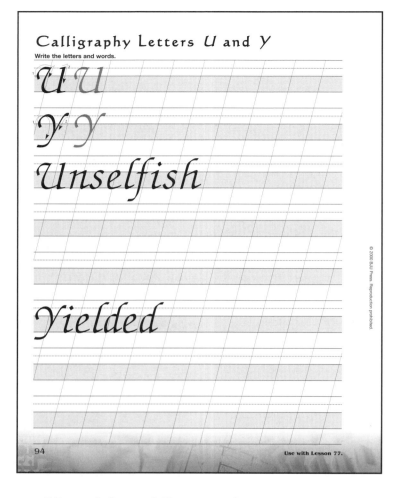

Materials and Preparation

Have available:

- A chisel-point pen for each student.
- A guide sheet for each student.
- Two pieces of typing paper for each student.
- A transparency of the advanced guide sheet.
- An overhead projector.
- An overhead pen.
- A Bible.
- Worktext page 94 for each student.

——— Lesson Content ———

Introduction

Direct a word study—Remind the students that one of the character qualities already presented is *generous*. Ask them to guess a related character quality beginning with *u*. *(unselfish)* Ask a student to read aloud Romans 6:13; then ask the students to guess another character quality from the

verse. *(yielded)* Elicit the meaning *(to be submissive to something)* and ask, "To whom should you be yielded?" *(to the Lord, to parents, to teachers, and to others in positions of authority)*

Skill development

Direct a warm-up activity—After distributing a piece of typing paper and a pen to each student, direct the class to write five of each practice stroke.

Demonstrate the formation of uppercase *U* and *Y*— Write the letters on the lines on the overhead, using the transparency guide and verbalizing the direction of each stroke as you write. Point out that there are no similarities between these two letters. Tell the students that the uppercase and the lowercase *U* are similar.

(1) Swing left and around, Drop and swing around right.
(2) Short diagonal right, Drop and glide right.

(1) Swing left and around to the right, Drop left and slide left.
(2) Glide left and drop left to lock.

Guided practice

Direct handwriting on worktext page 94—Point out the arrow that indicates the direction of each stroke. Direct the students to read the directions and complete the page.

Continued practice

Direct practice with typing paper and a guide sheet— Tell the students to use the advanced guide sheet as they practice the new letters and words on typing paper.

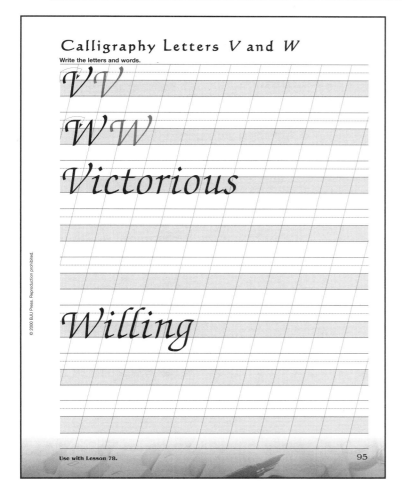

Calligraphy Letters *V* and *W*

Write the letters and words.

VV

WW

Victorious

Willing

Use with Lesson 78.   95

Materials and Preparation

Have available:

- A chisel-point pen for each student.
- A guide sheet for each student.
- Two pieces of typing paper for each student.
- A transparency of the advanced guide sheet.
- An overhead projector.
- An overhead pen.
- A copy of the hymn "I'll Go Where You Want Me to Go."

——— Lesson Content ———

Introduction

Lead a discussion—Tell the class that this lesson's character qualities are *victorious* and *willing*. Mention the title of the hymn "I'll Go Where You Want Me to Go" and ask how *victorious* and *willing* are illustrated in this thought. *(The Christian who is willing to go anywhere is going to be victorious in what he does because God will enable him.)* Lead the class in singing the hymn.

Skill development

Direct a warm-up activity—After distributing a piece of typing paper and a pen to each student, direct the class to write five of each practice stroke.

Demonstrate the formation of uppercase *V* and *W*— Write the letters on the lines on the overhead, using the transparency guide and verbalizing the direction of each stroke as you write. Show the students that uppercase *V* and *W* are similar. Point out that the *W*, better named *double V,* is almost like two *V*'s connected. Tell the students that as with the *A,* the difficult part of forming a *V* is making the letter look like it has a 13° slant when none of its strokes follow the 13° slant.

Swing left and around,
Drop,
Climb right high and curve
*   left.*

Swing left and around,
Drop,
Climb right,
Drop,
Climb right high and curve
*   left.*

Guided practice

Direct handwriting on worktext page 95—Direct the students to remove page 95 from their worktexts. Point out the arrow that indicates the direction of each stroke. Direct them to read the directions and complete the page.

Continued practice

Direct practice with typing paper and a guide sheet— Tell the students to use the advanced guide sheet as they practice the new letters and words on typing paper.

> The back of this page will be used in the next lesson.

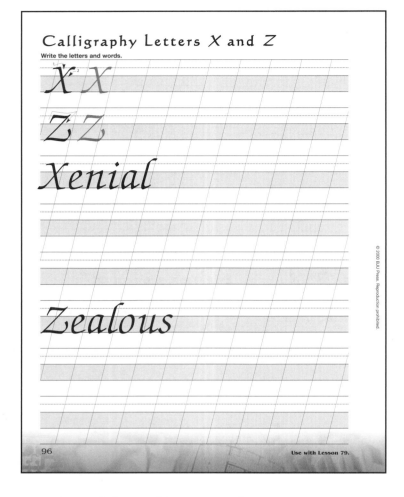

Calligraphy Letters *X* and *Z*

Write the letters and words.

X X

Z Z

Xenial

Zealous

96   Use with Lesson 79.

© 2000 BJU Press. Reproduction prohibited.

Materials and Preparation

Have available:

- A chisel-point pen for each student.
- A guide sheet for each student.
- Two pieces of typing paper for each student.
- A transparency of the advanced guide sheet.
- An overhead projector.
- An overhead pen.
- Worktext page 96 for each student.

——— Lesson Content ———

Introduction

Lead a discussion—*Xenial,* the character trait for the letter *x,* comes from a Greek word that means "guest." It refers to a friendly relationship between two persons from different countries. Explain this to the class and have them give synonyms that describe this attitude. *(friendly, hospitable, congenial)* Mention that the other character trait,

zealous (enthusiastic, devoted to an idea), is a trait that can be good or bad, depending on how it is directed. Ask the students for examples as time permits.

Skill development

Direct a warm-up activity—After distributing a piece of typing paper and a pen to each student, direct the class to write five of each practice stroke.

Demonstrate the formation of uppercase *X* and *Z*— Write the letters on the lines on the overhead, using the transparency guide and verbalizing the direction of each stroke as you write. Point out that these two letters are similar to their lowercase brothers. Remind the students to keep the first stroke of the *X* and the horizontal strokes of the *Z* fairly straight.

(1) Glide right,
    Drop right and glide
        right.
(2) Glide left,
    Drop left and glide left.

Short stroke up,
Glide right and slight
    curve,
Retrace and drop left,
Glide right and curve up.

Guided practice

Direct handwriting on worktext page 96—Point out the arrow that indicates the direction of each stroke. Direct the students to read the directions and complete the page.

Continued practice

Direct practice with typing paper and a guide sheet— Tell the students to use the advanced guide sheet as they practice the new letters and words on typing paper.

128

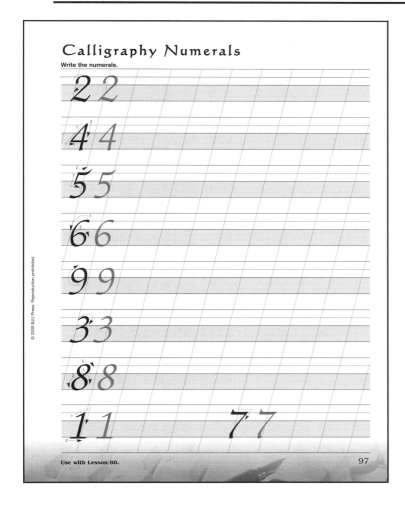

Calligraphy Numerals

Write the numerals.

2 2
4 4
5 5
6 6
9 9
3 3
8 8
1 1   7 7

Use with Lesson 80.   97

Materials and Preparation

Have available:

- A chisel-point pen for each student.
- A guide sheet for each student.
- Two pieces of typing paper for each student.
- A transparency of the advanced guide sheet.
- An overhead projector.
- An overhead pen.

——— Lesson Content ———

Introduction

Lead an activity—Point out to the students that many people throughout history (as well as today) have used numeral systems different from our system. For example, explain to the students that in 3000 B.C. Egyptians used *hieroglyphics* (picture writing) to write numerals. Give the students the Egyptian numeral system shown below.

1	/	Stroke
10	∩	Arch
100	9	Coiled Rope
1,000	ↄ	Lotus Flower
10,000	⌐	Finger
100,000	ↄ	Tadpole

Ask the students to convert the following numbers from the Egyptian numeral system to our numeral system.

99∩9∩∩/999∩// = 643

⌐⌐⌐ↄ9∩ↄↄ//ↄ////ↄↄ/// = 46,119

9∩9∩∩//∩∩∩/ = 263

ↄ⌐⌐ↄ9ↄ∩9⌐ↄ///ↄↄ/ = 134,214

Ask the students if they can figure out two ways that the Egyptian numeral system differs from our system and one way that it resembles our system. *(The Egyptian system did not have a zero, and the symbols could be written in any order since the value of a symbol did not depend on its position. The Egyptian system was based on 10.)*

Skill development

Direct a warm-up activity—After distributing a piece of typing paper and a pen to each student, direct the class to write five of each practice stroke.

Demonstrate the formation of the numerals—Write each numeral on the lines on the overhead, verbalizing the direction of each stroke as you write. Point out that the numerals use the same guidelines as the uppercase letters. Tell the students that a zero is the same as an uppercase *O*. If you have time, show them an alternate way of writing the *7* and *9*. Explain to the students that sometimes calligraphers start the *7* and *9* at the body line and go below the base line.

129

(1) Short diagonal right, Drop.
(2) Cross at bottom.

(1) Swing around to the left.
(2) Swing right and around to lock.

Swing up and around,
Drop left,
Glide right and hook.

Short diagonal left,
Glide right,
Drop left,
Curve right.

Swing up and around to the left,
Retrace and swing around to the left.

(1) Swing down,
Swerve around and back.
(2) Swing left and around to lock.
(3) Swing right and around to lock.

(1) Drop left,
Glide right.
(2) Drop.

Swing around left and up and around,
Swing down low to the left.

(1) Drop below body line and swing around.
(2) Glide right and curve up.

Guided practice

Direct handwriting on worktext page 97—Tell the students to remove page 97 from their worktexts. Point out the arrow that indicates the direction of each stroke. Ask them to read the directions and complete the page.

Continued practice

Direct practice with typing paper and a guide sheet—Tell the students to use the advanced guide sheet as they practice the new letters and words on typing paper.

The back of this page will be used in the next lesson.

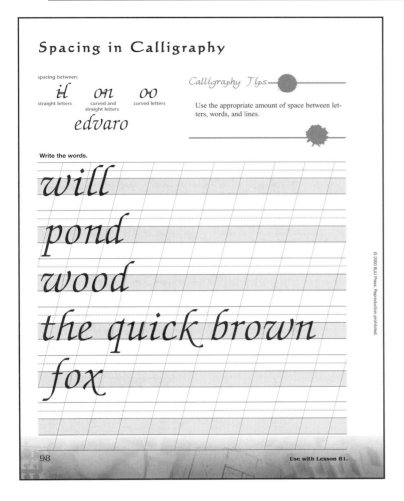

Skill development

Direct a warm-up activity—After distributing a piece of typing paper and a pen to each student, direct the class to write five of each practice stroke.

Guided practice

Direct handwriting on worktext page 98—Point out that the words *will, pond,* and *wood* on the page are included so that the students can practice spacing within a word and that the phrase *the quick brown fox* is included so that they can practice spacing between words and between lines. Direct the students to complete the page.

Walk around the classroom to check that the students are making the correct strokes for the letters. Look for common errors.

Continued practice

Direct practice with typing paper and a guide sheet—Tell the students to use the advanced guide sheet as they write a verse or part of a verse on typing paper. Remind them to observe the spacing rules.

Materials and Preparation

Have available:

- A chisel-point pen for each student.
- A guide sheet for each student.
- Two pieces of typing paper for each student.
- A transparency of the advanced guide sheet.
- An overhead projector.
- An overhead pen.
- Worktext page 98 for each student.

—— Lesson Content ——

Introduction

Lead a discussion about the spacing rules—Write the phrase *the quick brown fox* from worktext page 98 on the overhead. Use poor spacing between letters, words, and lines. Ask the students to name the three spacing rules; then point out the problems in your example.

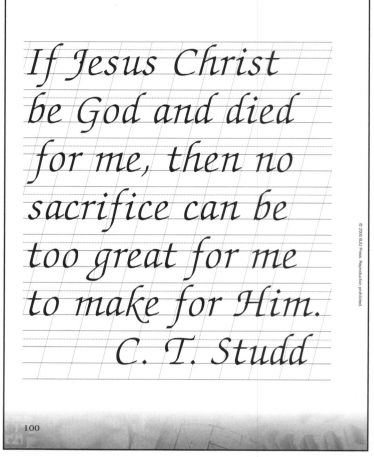

Materials and Preparation

Have available:

- A chisel-point pen for each student.
- A guide sheet for each student.
- Two pieces of typing paper for each student.
- A transparency of the advanced guide sheet.
- An overhead projector.
- An overhead pen.
- Adding-machine tape (about five feet for each student).
- A pair of scissors for each student.

—— Lesson Content ——

Introduction

Direct a discussion from page 99—Direct the students' attention to page 99 in their worktexts. Ask them to point out which layout example they think is better and why they think it is better. *(The one on the right is better because of good planning: the calligrapher did not run out of room in the middle of a word; it has equal margins on both sides; and it has a slightly larger margin at the top than the other one does.)*

Skill development

Direct a warm-up activity—After distributing a piece of typing paper and a pen to each student, direct the class to write five of each practice stroke.

Guided practice

Direct an activity using worktext page 99—Give each student about five feet of adding-machine tape (strips of paper will work just as well). Direct the class to write the saying on page 99 on the adding-machine tape. Ask the students to cut the tape apart between each word and to arrange the words in a layout that would fit on a piece of typing paper. Then tell them to write the saying in that layout format on a piece of typing paper, using the guide sheet.

Walk around the classroom to check that the students are making the correct strokes for the letters.

Continued practice

Have the students practice with typing paper and a guide sheet—Have the students choose a verse, poem, or saying from pages 100-103 and write it in the layout format shown. Then direct the students to design their own layout of a famous saying or verse and letter it.

Direct the students to write a tribute to honor someone special—Tell the students that a tribute is a gift or service showing respect, gratitude, or affection. Tell each student to think of a person whom he would like to honor. Direct him to imagine the person's general appearance, typical expressions, and responses. When he has the qualities of that person in mind, ask him to write a letter, build an acrostic on the letters in the person's name or occupation, or write the person's qualities or services in the form of a certificate. Direct him to do this activity in Chancery cursive.

Photograph Credits

The following agencies and individuals have furnished materials to meet the photographic needs of this textbook. We wish to express our gratitude to them for their important contribution.

George R. Collins
Corel Corporation
NASA (National Aeronautics and Space Administration)
NIH (National Institutes of Health)
PhotoDisc, Inc.
USDA (United States Department of Agriculture)

Unusual Films
Ward's Natural Science Establishment, Inc.
Dawn L. Watkins
www.arttoday.com

Cover
George R. Collins: Lighthouse; Corel Corporation: Space stars, Woman pilot; PhotoDisc, Inc.: Astronomer, Gears, Helicopter, Nurse, Satellite dish, Xylographer

Page 3
Corel Corporation: Stars (background); PhotoDisc, Inc.: Astronomer, Calligrapher and calligraphy pen

Page 9
Corel Corporation: Rocks, Rock texture; PhotoDisc, Inc.: Diver, Starfish, Surveyor

Page 15
Corel Corporation: Marble background; PhotoDisc, Inc.: Blueprint, Engineer, Geologist, Quartz; Ward's Natural Science Establishment, Inc.: Gems

Page 21
PhotoDisc, Inc.: Courthouse, Gavel, Inventor, Judge; www.arttoday.com: Invention device

Page 27
Corel Corporation: Toothbrush; PhotoDisc, Inc.: Dentist, Large x-ray, Surgeon; www.arttoday.com: Small x-ray

Page 33
Corel Corporation: Fish background, Fish fly; PhotoDisc, Inc.: Fisherman, Tailor, Thread

Page 39
George R. Collins: Large lighthouse; Corel Corporation: Lighthouse keeper, Small lighthouse, Tulips; PhotoDisc, Inc.: Leaf, Sky; United States Department of Agriculture (USDA): Botanist

Page 45
Corel Corporation: Apples; PhotoDisc, Inc.: Crayons, Horticulturist; Unusual Films: Teacher

Page 51
National Aeronautics and Space Administration (NASA): Hurricane; National Institutes of Health (NIH): Nurse and boy; PhotoDisc, Inc.: Nurse; Unusual Films: Meteorologist

Page 57
Corel Corporation: Woman pilot; National Aeronautics and Space Administration (NASA): Cockpit; PhotoDisc, Inc.: Helicopter, Radio tower; Unusual Films: Radiobroadcasters

Page 63
Corel Corporation: Wood background; PhotoDisc, Inc.: Cat, Veterinarian; Unusual Films: Carving tools, Xylographer lady, Xylographer man

Page 69
Corel Corporation: Baseball; Digital Stock: Umpire; PhotoDisc, Inc.: Baseball field; Dawn L. Watkins: Watchmaker and watch

Page 75
Corel Corporation: Yacht, Yachtsman; PhotoDisc, Inc.: Lion cub, Zoologist; www.arttoday.com: Zoo

Page 81
PhotoDisc, Inc.: Boy and teacher, Girls, School road; Unusual Films: Open Bible

PhotoDisc, Inc.: Green collage on all People and Professions unit openers and purple collage on Character Quality

Photos on inside pages are credited individually.

Appendix

Dear Parents,

This year your child will be using the sixth-grade materials of the *HANDWRITING for Christian Schools*® program, which uses a unique style of writing developed by Bob Jones University Press. This program seeks to lay a foundation of writing skills on which early learning is broadened and reinforced, not replaced.

Since this may be the last year of formal handwriting instruction for many children, each unit has a lesson that uses self-evaluation techniques. As a parent you may want to pay special attention to those pages. (They are identified by a small grid that the student will fill in as he examines his own work.)

While *HANDWRITING 6 for Christian Schools* thoroughly reviews basic letter forms and skills, it also places a strong emphasis on motivation. It presents alternate styles of capital letters to stimulate interest at a time when personal handwriting habits usually begin to deteriorate and when students have a natural tendency to develop their own unique letter styles. By continuing to teach the concepts of consistency and readability while showing alternate letter styles, *HANDWRITING 6* gives students an opportunity to build a personal style that can become a lifetime communication tool. The theme of the student text, *People and Professions,* also has a high motivational appeal to preadolescents.

Still another motivational aspect of the sixth-grade program is its emphasis on calligraphy. Throughout the school year your sixth-grader will be introduced to some basic concepts of this special type of printing. Early in the school year lessons on the lowercase Chancery letters will be interspersed with regular handwriting lessons. To avoid loss or overuse of the calligraphy pens, I will keep them between lessons. Otherwise the pens might not be available for the final series of lessons when the students will learn the uppercase Chancery letters and have an opportunity to prepare a project. Please remember that the goal of the calligraphy work is motivational rather than a mastery of calligraphy.

The basic cursive alphabet, as well as the numerals that your child will use in sixth grade, are given on the back of this letter for your information. The arrows on the letters and numerals indicate the direction of the strokes. This may be a valuable tool for you as you monitor your child's handwriting progress.

Thank you for your support and your help at home.

Sincerely,

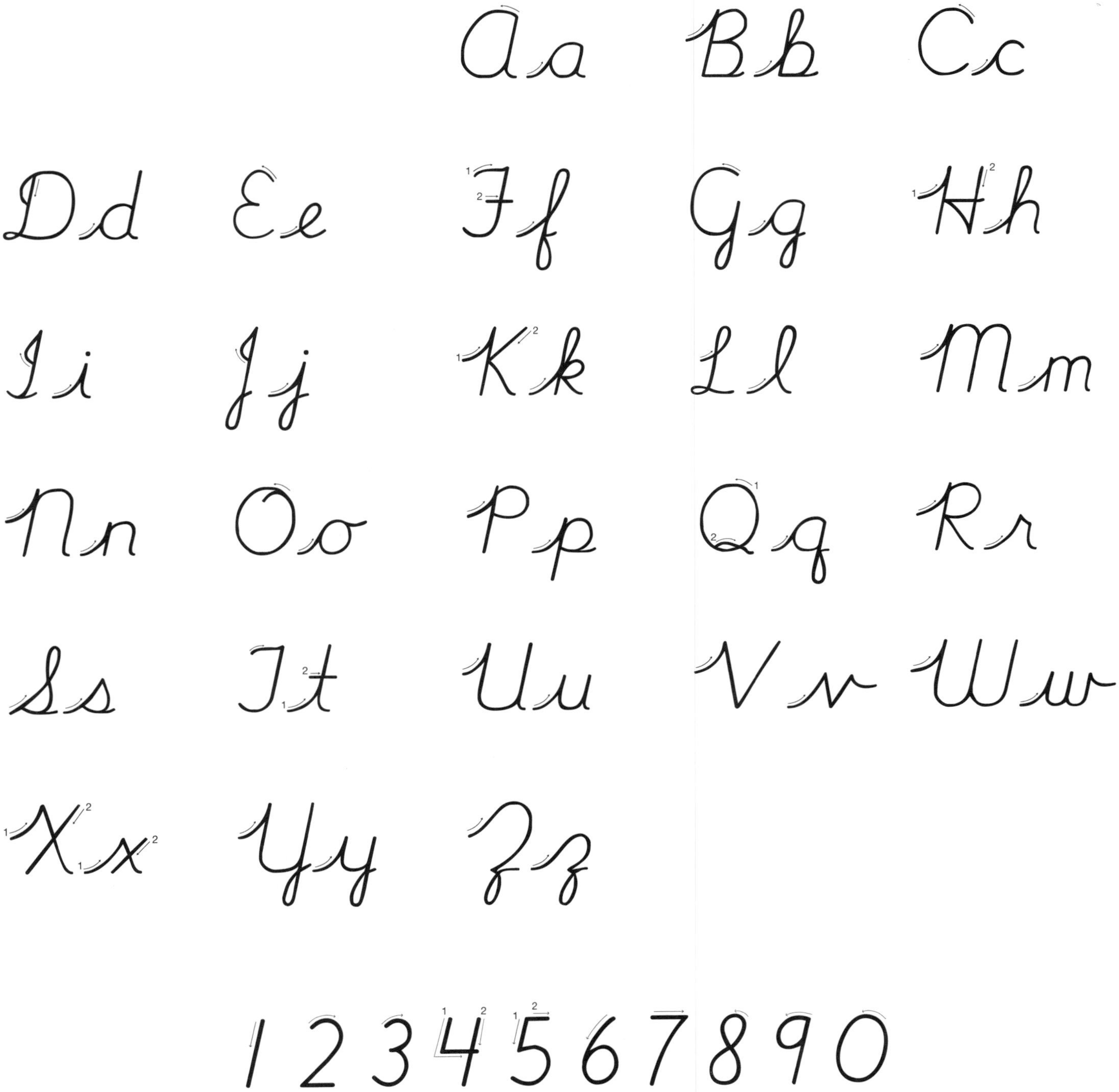

Aa Bb Cc
Dd Ee Ff Gg Hh
Ii Jj Kk Ll Mm
Nn Oo Pp Qq Rr
Ss Tt Uu Vv Ww
Xx Yy Zz

1 2 3 4 5 6 7 8 9 0

Bulletin Boards

You can prepare good bulletin boards. Design your bulletin boards to extend the lesson themes in *HANDWRITING 6 for Christian Schools* and to provide opportunities to display excellent handwriting efforts.

You can easily enlarge the sample bulletin boards that follow. If you have access to an opaque projector, it is a simple tracing process. An overhead projector will also work. Simply make a transparency of the page and trace the projection.

If you do not have access to projection equipment, you can enlarge the figures by using the grid method of enlargement. Draw a grid of one-inch squares on the picture you wish to enlarge. Draw another grid on a separate piece of paper, but enlarge the squares proportionately. (For example, if you want your enlargement to be twice as large, make the squares two inches on each side.) Then copy the figure square by square onto the enlarged grid.

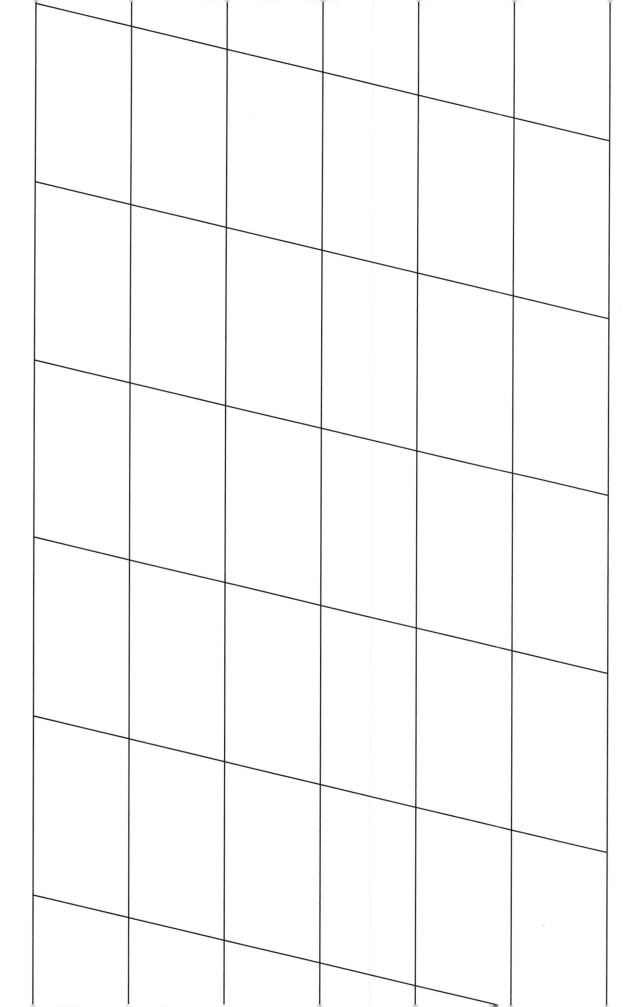

Lowercase Guide Sheet

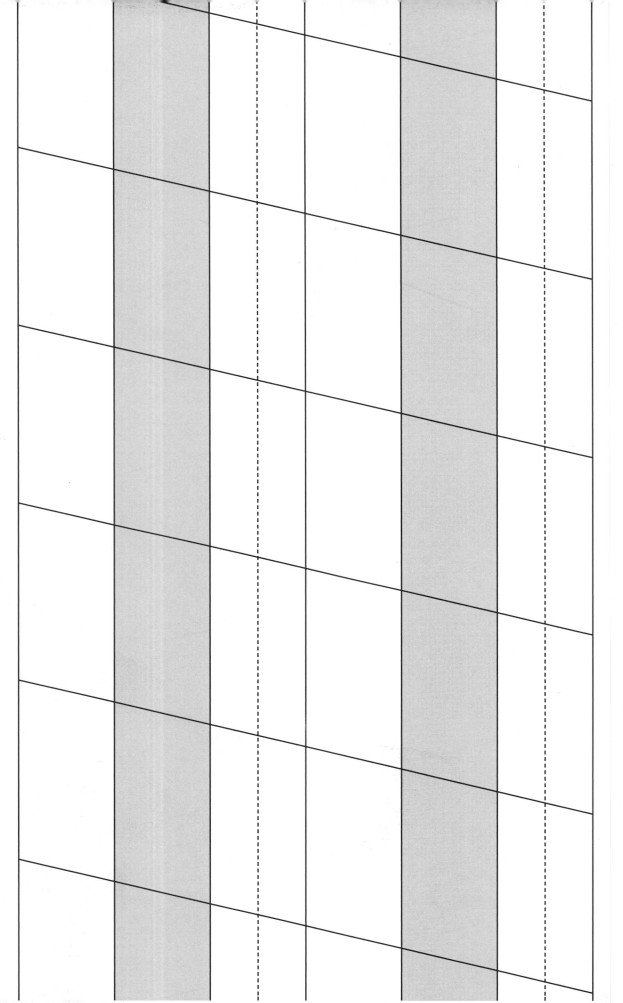

Evaluation

Name: _____

Date: _____

	Satisfactory	Shows Improvement	Needs Improvement	Suggestions for Improvement
1. Posture				
2. Paper Positioning				
3. Pencil Hold				
4. Letter Formation				
5. Alignment				
6. Slant				
7. Spacing				
8. Neatness				

Glossary

alignment—the correct placement of letters in relation to the base line

base line—the line on which the written letters rest

bounce—the ending of the stroke for the lowercase *f* and *q* that leads to the connecting of the cursive letter that follows

cursive stroke—the stroke that differentiates many PreCursive letters from their counterpart cursive letters; serves as the connecting stroke between most letters

curve—the ending of the stroke of most PreCursive and cursive letters

descenders—the portion of certain letters that descends below the base line

loop—to cross a part of the letter already written with a high, sweeplike stroke

lowercase letters—uncapitalized letters

midline—the line of dashes found between the top line and base line

one o'clock letters—letters beginning at the one o'clock position as compared to a clock; found in uppercase and lowercase *a, c, g, o, q,* and in uppercase *e*

retrace—backtracking along a part of the letter already written

rhythm—regularity of pressure patterns of fingers on the writing instrument

serif—a slight curve at the end of many letters

slant—the 5- to 15-degree tilt of letters

spacing—the amount of distance between letters and words and the arrangement of writing on the page

sweep out—the ending of a stroke that moves outward from left to right, connecting to letters that follow in a word; found in uppercase *b* and *i* and lowercase *b, o, p, s, v,* and *w*

top line—the uppermost portion of a handwriting line; the line above the midline

uppercase letters—capitalized letters